THE RIDER FROM HELL

The Sobering Story of a Psychopathic Cyclist

ARNOLD LOXLEY

Text copyright ©2018 Arnold Loxley

The author has asserted his moral right under the Copyright, Designs and Patents Act, 1988, to be identified as the author of this work.

All rights reserved. No part of this publication may be reproduced, stored in a retrieval system, or transmitted, in any form or by any means, without the prior permission in writing of the publisher.

1

"How do you feel, Carl?"

"Good."

"I was sorry to hear about your father passing away."

"Thanks. I was glad I was out by then, so I could arrange the funeral and so on."

"Yes. I... er, guess this changes your circumstances quite a lot."

"That's right. Now I don't have to look for the job that I'd never have found anyway."

"Oh, I don't know, and if you still–"

"No bullshit, please, Mike," Carl said to his probation officer. "You know as well as I do that a convicted murderer who's been inside for sixteen years would never find a job in a month of Sundays... in a *year* of Sundays."

Mike scratched a sideburn and gazed at the pale, stocky, mild-looking man of forty-three sitting opposite him. "It's been known to happen, though it's true that it's not easy. You'd have a chance, I think, as you're just about the most rehabilitated... ex-prisoner I've seen for a long time. You've got glowing reports from inside and I for one will give you a great reference."

"Thanks, Mike, but I don't need to work. Besides the house, my dad left me a packet in savings and bonds and stuff. I'm still trying to get my head round it now." He shook his head of wavy brown hair and laughed pleasantly.

"You'll have to do something to occupy your time though. You'd be best to steer clear of your old friends and try to make some new ones."

"Most of my old friends are dead or in the nick. I'd not go near them anyway. No booze or drugs for me from now on. I feel I've got energy to burn. Maybe I'll take up gardening or something."

"Has the house got much of a garden?"

"Yes, about half a football pitch." He chuckled and shook his head. "My parents worked hard and had high hopes for me, then I messed up. Shame they're not alive to see that I've changed."

"Your dad did, didn't he?"

"Hmm, yes, but he was too far gone to notice much, poor sod." Carl focused his sharp blue eyes on a dusty paperclip and sighed. "Gardening though, I don't know. I'm not sure it's for me, and the gardener I've got is a sound enough bloke. Maybe I need to do something more energetic." He prodded his modest paunch. "I'd like to get rid of this."

"You could join a gym. That way you'd meet people too," Mike said brightly. He'd been a probation officer for eight of his thirty-two years and the job was already wearing him down. He was glad to have been assigned to Carl, who he'd be seeing periodically for the next couple of years, as he at least proved that the prison system did work from time to time. Carl had entered a high security jail as a drug-addled psycho who'd stabbed a dealer to death and come out of an open prison with a sheaf of qualifications, a clean bill of health and an apparently positive mental state. The inheritance would help, of course, and as long as this agreeable, straight-talking man could find something to occupy his time, Mike anticipated many pleasant, stress-free meetings to punctuate his otherwise irksome daily grind.

"Hmm, no, not the gym. It'd remind me of being inside, as I used the ones there, though not as much as I should have. I don't like groups of people anyway. I prefer to meet folk one to one. I don't know, maybe I'll start jogging or something."

"How about cycling?"

"Haven't been on a bike since I was a kid."

Mike leant his sinewy arms on the desk and smiled brightly at Carl. "That's my hobby. I ride with a local club. I'd go mad in this job if I didn't have my weekend rides."

Carl, somewhat taken aback by this sudden surge of enthusiasm, grinned and said that he wasn't sure if he'd still be able to ride one.

"Of course you will. Riding a bike is like... everything else." He cleared his throat. "It's a great way to see the countryside and it's not as hard to get into as running. If you take it slowly at first you'll soon find you can go further and faster. I don't normally mention it here, because... well, most of them would laugh at me, and besides, bikes and the gear cost money and I don't like to suggest something they wouldn't be able to afford, but you don't have that problem.

Once you get into it you could join my club. Here we're not supposed to associate with… er, clients, but there'd be nothing to stop you joining. They're a great bunch of blokes, and a few women, mostly attached, and no-one'd need to know about your… er, background. Sorry, I get carried away when I start talking about cycling."

Carl chuckled. "You obviously like it a lot."

"I love it. Next month when it stays light longer I'll be out some evenings too. It's a bit of a drug, I suppose, but a good one."

"All those endorphins, eh? Ha, I suppose it'd be a kind of therapy."

"That's right. You can't beat it for letting off steam. What do you say?"

"I'm interested. How much should I spend on a bike?"

"Oh, a thousand quid at the most. Then you'll be able to buy a better one if you get really keen. I can recommend a good bike shop. If you say I sent you they might knock a bit off." He looked at his watch.

"Are we almost done?"

"What? No, we've a while yet. I was just wondering if I could squeeze in a ride when I get home. The wife won't mind me having dinner afterwards, I hope. So, have you got to grips with all your paperwork and things…?"

Half an hour later Carl left the building feeling intrigued by this cycling business. His four-bedroom house on the edge of town was on a leafy lane which led to more lanes, so if he did decide to have a go he wouldn't have much traffic to contend with, hurtling cars being a major downside of cycling in his opinion. Instead of driving straight home in the Volvo he'd inherited from his father, he dropped by a large second-hand shop and enquired about pushbikes. The bland young assistant pointed him to the rear of the shop, where he found a motley assortment of clean but well-used machines. Among them was a red mountain bike which looked about the right size for his five foot nine inch frame. He liked the colour, but was a bit surprised by the price tag of £190, as the other bikes were all under a hundred.

"Why's that red bike so dear?" he asked the lad.

He put his phone down. "Oh, it's a Trek. The others are all pretty rubbish, but that's a good one; cost about six hundred new, the bloke said."

"I'll give you one-seventy for it," he said.

"I'm not allowed to lower the price."

Carl gazed mildly at the youngster. "Oh, come on, this is a second hand shop. I bet you haggle plenty when you buy stuff."

The boy's Adam's apple rose and fell. There was something a bit creepy about this guy, pleasant though he seemed, so he said he could let it go for £180.

"That'll do. Can you wrap it up, please?"

"Eh?" he said, involuntarily reaching for his phone.

"It's a joke."

"Oh, ha, right."

"Here you are. Better count it."

"That's right, thanks," he said, before watching the thickset man wheel the bike out of the shop, glad that he'd gone.

After a bit of fiddling Carl managed to get the front wheel out of the bike and slide the surprisingly light machine into the back of the car. On arriving home he reassembled it, adjusted the saddle and rode up and down the long driveway, shakily at first, as at the open prison bicycles had been conspicuous by their absence. It must have been twenty-odd years since he'd last mounted one, as from the age of seventeen sporting activities had taken a backseat in favour of less salubrious pastimes. When he'd gained more confidence he headed out onto the lane and rode up a slope which he knew to be about half a mile long. Once he'd worked out the gears it felt good to spin the pedals between the hedgerows, but remembering that he hadn't locked the car he turned around at the top and coasted back to the house, where he spent the next two hours indulging his recently acquired passion for the internet, that wonderful font of all knowledge which he'd used only under the strictest supervision during the last year of his sentence as part of his re-insertion sessions.

As well as oil, a pump and a water bottle, which he'd already pencilled onto his mental list, he discovered that he also needed spare inner tubes, a few basic tools and a bag to put them in, not to mention a helmet and suitable clothing, though he couldn't see himself in lycra just yet. After a slightly longer ride along the lane he had a bite to eat before driving down to the bike shop which Mike had recommended. After buying what he required he began to browse the array of road and mountain bikes, upon which a lithe young lady sidled over to ask him what he was looking for.

"Oh, I'm just browsing now, but... well, I might buy a road bike at some point," he said, having instinctively avoided mentioning Mike's name, as in prison he'd learnt to be sparing with the information he divulged.

"We've got a good selection here, but we can get just about any model on the market. We finance them too."

"How much is that red one hanging up there?"

"The Wilier? Just under four thousand."

"Bloody hell, that much?"

"Yes, but's it's a top racing bike. You don't need to spend anywhere near that amount to get a really good bike."

"What could I get for a thousand?" he asked, enjoying his proximity to the pretty woman. Maybe when he got into shape he'd begin to try his luck with the ladies, but he was in no hurry, as he'd got used to his own company.

She showed him a couple of cheaper models which looked almost as flashy as the Wilier and he promised to return when he felt he deserved a better bike.

"I've just taken up cycling, you see, so I'm going to ride an old mountain bike until I get fit, or fitter," he said, observing her response to his pleasantries.

"That's a good idea. If I were you I'd do about five hundred miles on that before you buy something better."

"That sounds a lot, and how can I measure the distance? On the map, I suppose."

She raised her manicured brows and smiled. "Get a GPS app on your phone."

"A... oh, yes, I'll do that."

"Or a cycle computer, so you can watch the total grow. That'll be satisfying."

"I'll have one of those then."

She showed him a selection and he chose a basic model.

"I wonder how long it'll take me to do five hundred miles," he said once he'd paid.

"That depends on how often you get out and how far you go. Maybe a couple of months."

"A couple of months, yes, I think I can do that. Well, I'll see you when I've done the first five hundred," he said, venturing a broad smile for the first time.

She smiled back. "OK, I look forward to seeing you then."

"Bye, and thanks."

On arriving home he read the instructions, attached the computer and sensor, locked the door, and set off up the lane once more. This time he crested the rise and freewheeled down the other side, before labouring up another slope until his legs began to sweat inside his jeans. Having covered three miles he began to turn in the lane when a blue van hurtled around the bend and had to brake sharply to avoid hitting him.

"Fucking clown!" shouted the young driver, to which Carl responded with an apologetic wave. He'd have to be more careful, he reflected as he rode back, the frequency of passing cars having increased, and he ought to avoid being out during the rush hour, as on such a narrow lane the drivers couldn't help but pass him closely, although most of them seemed considerate.

Of all the new sensations he'd experienced during his first real bike ride, the one that stuck with him after he'd showered was his having kept his cool when the van driver had abused him. He was pleased about that. Had he shown such restraint from the word go in the nick he could have been out after ten years, but it had taken him a long time to manage his anger and avoid the impulse to lash out at anyone who offended him. That driver had been his first test in the real world and he'd passed with flying colours. There'd been adrenalin and danger, but he'd still kept calm. He cracked open a can of coke and smiled in the kitchen mirror.

"You're a new man, Carl Coulton, or you will be when you've got rid of that flab," he said, before flashing his teeth and admiring his three brand new crowns.

2

The first hundred miles were the hardest and took him just a week, not once straying from the hilly but tranquil local lanes. On the seventh day it rained but, determined to complete the last dozen miles, he grinned and bore the downpour which left him soaked from head to foot. Although his cycling occupied a little over an hour of each morning – as much as his protesting legs could manage – he found himself so hooked on his new hobby that he spent many more researching all that pertained to it. As well as looking into all the gear he'd require, he also read about the different ways people enjoyed the sport. Some folk were all-out racers, others pretended to be, while many more eschewed speed in favour of covering longer distances and exploring pastures new. These called themselves touring cyclists and as each day passed he found himself increasingly drawn to this more relaxed and, he reckoned, rewarding way of riding. From his home he'd be able to explore the Ribble Valley and the Forest of Bowland, while a short drive would put the whole of the Yorkshire Dales within reach.

Once he'd explored those places thoroughly he could go further afield and maybe make multi-day trips, stopping at B&Bs and meeting people along the way. No-one would ever imagine that this trim, bronzed cyclist had spent over a third of his life in prison, as who'd ever heard of a drug-addled assassin puffing and sweating his way up a mountain pass? Yes, he'd become Carl the Cycle Tourist, a bit obsessed by his hobby, perhaps, but a more healthy, carefree and harmless – above all harmless – fellow you couldn't wish to meet!

Before he could equip himself fittingly for his future exploits there was the small matter of another four hundred miles to ride on the sluggish old Trek. After several calamitous years in the nick something had finally clicked inside his thick head and he'd learnt to toe the line and set himself goals. Once he'd seen the light and begun to avoid his more disreputable companions, success had soon followed; more rewarding jobs, GCSE studies, two A levels and a foundation degree in history. He'd achieved all that by setting himself goals and sticking to them, so despite an almost irresistible impulse to splash out on a top-notch touring bike right away, he resolved to ride the whole five hundred miles on his chunky-tyred steed before returning to the bike shop.

After a day's rest he decided to double his daily mileage for a week, but this meant heading west beyond the peaceful lanes to the small town of Whalley, from where he'd soon reach another network of minor roads. The first time he crossed the busy bypass, negotiated the compact but chaotic town centre and covered another three fairly hectic miles, he gripping the handlebars tightly and winced each time a vehicle passed him, but he soon came to realise that most of the drivers gave him a wide berth and none got closer than three or four feet. He still felt relieved when the traffic thinned and after a few enjoyable miles along almost deserted roads he faced the return journey with a new mindset.

"As long as I ride straight and stick to the side of the road I don't need to give the cars so much as a thought," he muttered to himself as he descended into Whalley. "And at this mini-roundabout I'm going to assert myself and imagine I'm in the car... there, you see, you soft git, if you ride properly there's nothing to worry about, except that bloody big hill back to the bypass, but that problem's in the legs rather than in the mind."

Carl's odometer registered twenty-eight miles as he crested the last rise before descending to his house, so he decided to turn around and clock another two, despite his weary legs and empty stomach.

What a cruel twist of fate that unnecessary addition to his so-far satisfactory ride proved to be, for no sooner had he begun to coast down the slope than a Nissan Micra which had begun to overtake him was forced to pull in sharply to avoid an oncoming van, missing Carl's handlebar end and front wheel by a matter of inches, before trundling away as if nothing untoward had occurred. Carl felt a rush of blood to the head and roared at the oblivious driver, before stamping on the pedals in pursuit of his prey. When the car indicated left and slowed to enter a driveway his wrath turned to glee as he applied the brakes, but when he perceived the driver's coiffured white hair his mood changed to one of perplexity. He'd intended to put the fear of God into the bastard who'd almost wiped him out, but faced with the prospect of squaring up to a little old lady, he found himself laughing out loud, mostly from relief, he later realised.

Back in the day he might have threatened her with the handy razorblade he often used to carry, but the rehabilitated Carl Coulson concluded that a friendly word in her ear would be more appropriate, for he felt compelled to point out the error of her ways.

"Excuse me," he said when she'd struggled out of the car.

"Yes?" she replied, a momentary look of alarm soon turning to one of enquiry, as this was just one of those sweaty cyclists one saw so often these days.

"Er, I don't know if you realise that you almost knocked me off my bike just now," he said almost apologetically.

"Me?"

"Yes, just now when you overtook me and had to pull in."

"Oh, that van, yes. Was I too close?"

Carl, still straddling his bike, smiled and indicated a short distance between finger and thumb.

"Ooh, so close? I *am* sorry, young man. I had no idea."

"Didn't you?" he asked, partly to himself.

"Of course not. Oh, I wish people wouldn't drive so fast, don't you?"

"Yes."

She approached him, still wearing a concerned expression, but only to open the boot. Thus it was that Carl ended up helping his erstwhile foe to carry her shopping bags to the front door where, after pointing out that he was a near-neighbour, he politely declined the offer of a cup of tea and set off to doggedly complete his thirty miles, his ear cocked for approaching cars like never before.

During the rest of the day his mind returned to the incident countless times and he convinced himself that even if the driver had been a man of half the old dear's age, he'd have restricted himself to a few choice expletives before going on his way. Carl was handy with his fists – he'd had to be – but he knew full well that were he to employ them in earnest he could find himself back inside in the twinkling of an eye. That, however, oughtn't to be the sole reason for avoiding violence. He'd learnt to control himself in prison, despite appearing cowardly at times, and he *must* carry on the good work on the outside if he were to stand a chance of leading a fulfilling life.

There was something else that bothered him about the near miss too though; the fact that the old lady truly hadn't realised how close she'd come to landing him in the hedge. She wouldn't be the only motorist he'd come across whose vision and reflexes were past their best, but after weighing up this potential danger for some time he concluded that if you shield yourself from all of life's perils, you miss out on a lot of things. The drink, drugs and violence must have used up over half of his nine lives, but surely he had a few left with which to enjoy his new passion.

"Thousands… no, millions of others enjoy cycling," he said to the mirror. "And you're not going to be put off by a bit of risk."

The following morning he shoved the bike into the car and drove to Whalley. It wasn't something he intended to do every time, but he felt that he deserved a treat after his close shave and brow-beating afternoon, so he rode from there to the pretty village of Chipping and back and clocked another twenty-five incident-free miles. The thing was to be aware of potential danger, he concluded as he relived the near miss for the twentieth time. On hearing the approaching van he should have slowed down or even pulled over, he concluded, before visualising hypothetical scrapes as he rode and anticipating how he would react. He was a rookie cyclist, after all, and an experienced one, like Mike, would have foreseen the danger and taken action. Yes, that was it, once he'd improved his traffic-awareness he'd be fine, he thought as he logged the miles in his diary, prior to taking the cold bath that one hardy cycling blogger had recommended.

The lanes between Whalley and Chipping turned into his regular pedal-stomping ground for the next fortnight and just twenty-four days after his fortuitous conversation with Mike he returned to the bike shop and was delighted to find the same pretty assistant awaiting him.

"I've... er... done the five hundred miles," he told her.

"Yes, I guessed you might have," she said with a grin.

"Oh, why?"

"Well, you've lost weight and gained colour. You *look* like a cyclist now."

Carl blushed and cleared his throat. "So... well, I think I'm ready to buy a decent bike now."

"That's good."

"I'm going to go for a touring bike. I reckon that's the sort of cycling I want to do."

"OK. Let's see, we've got two in with medium frames, but we can have lots of other models here within a week or so."

Carl pictured the chunky mountain bike tyres that he'd worked so hard to turn around and hoped that he'd like one of the bikes in stock. One proved to be a grey Dawes Galaxy which seemed heavy but cost only £700, while the other was a maroon Ridgeback model which felt lighter but was priced at almost £1500.

"I like this one, but is it really twice as good as the other?" he asked.

"Oh, yes, the components are much better quality. You could ride around the world on this and only have to change the tyres, chain and brake blocks. So are you going to do real touring?"

"Yes, I think so, once I'm fit enough," he said, meeting her gaze and trying to gauge if she liked him. She wore no rings, but no, apart from being way too young for him it would be madness to try to date a local woman, as she'd find out about his past sooner or later. He glanced down at the matt-black triple chainset and imagined himself meeting an eligible lady miles away from Lancashire, maybe another cyclist with whom love would blossom as he helped her to repair a puncture…

"It's got really low gears, just like a mountain bike, so you'll get up anything on her," the ineligible lady said.

"Yes, and mudguards too. I'll take it. I'd like some bags for it, please."

"I'll show you some rear panniers that fit the rack."

"Right. I'd also like some of those clip-in pedals and some shoes, please, and… well, anything else you think I'll need for a week-long trip," he said, having rejected his initial idea of popping in regularly for bits and bobs, as the lovely girl would only put inadvisable ideas into his head. An ex-con with no wish to disclose his sordid past simply has to play away from home, he thought as he followed her over to the clothing racks, and half an hour later he walked out of the shop over two grand poorer, but equipped with everything he could possibly need, or so he thought at the time.

Once home he grabbed a bite to eat before pulling on his new black shorts and expensive yellow jacket, stepping into his SPD shoes and riding up and down the drive until he was sure he could unclip his feet without falling off. He felt like a spoilt child at Christmas when he set off up the lane and he really wished his parents could have seen him in his new getup on that fine machine. It would have reminded them of his fifteenth birthday when they'd presented him with a Raleigh racing bike, which he'd sold for fifty quid three years later in order to score some crack cocaine.

"All in the past," he muttered breathlessly as he powered up the slope like never before. Oh yes, *this* was a bike, and he'd put five thousand miles on its computer before the year was out or his name wasn't Carl Coulson, intrepid cycling machine and all-round good guy!

3

On that maiden twenty-mile ride he felt like the real McCoy and sensed that the motorists treated him with more respect than when he'd been wrestling with the mountain bike, his baggy shorts billowing in the breeze. Now they could see he was a proper cyclist with a smart bike, lycra shorts, a brightly coloured top and flashing LED lights, not just a wally bobbing up and down on an off-road bike. He was able to ride more smoothly, as befit a man in his forties, and he almost imagined the drivers doffing their caps as they eased past him. When he arrived home he hoped that he'd soon manage to put his traffic anxieties behind him and be able to concentrate on the joys of his new pursuit, so after showering and eating a healthy meal he settled down at the computer to plan more ambitious routes.

The mid-May forecast was fine so he decided to drive to Whalley and cycle over the Trough of Bowland the following day, returning by way of Scorton and Chipping. At fifty miles the route was a third longer than his previous best, but he trusted that his lighter bike would enable him to manage it easily, provided he had a few short breaks. Many cyclists, he knew, liked to stop off for a meal en route, but the thought of clumping into a twee café in his cycling gear didn't appeal to him at all. Better to fill two water bottles and take plenty of snacks which he could eat when he spotted somewhere nice to stop, he decided, and so it was that after an enjoyable first leg he sat down on a bench near Dunsop Bridge and munched a cereal bar while soaking up the benign sunshine.

After a long climb from Bashall Eaves he'd whooshed down a steep descent into the hamlet of Whitewell, from where the road had flattened as he followed the River Hodder up the picturesque valley. Although he knew the Trough of Bowland was going to be his toughest climb yet, he felt so elated and energised that he could hardly wait to stash the wrapper in his pocket and set off again. On the sinuous road the scenery became even more stunning as the valley gradually narrowed, and after briefly lamenting that he ought to have done things like this twenty-odd years ago, he steeled himself for the last and steepest part of the famous climb. As he engaged bottom gear – for he knew his limitations – he heard the first car for ages and sensed that it was coming up fast.

No matter, he thought as he grasped the bars and strove to stay in the saddle, it'll soon be past and the sound of my own breathing is all that I'll hear. As the road was so narrow he wasn't altogether surprised when the high-revving engine suddenly slowed behind him, but he wished they'd get a move on, as the thump-thump of their dratted music was getting on his nerves. Despite being almost at his limit he managed to raise his right hand from the bars to usher them past, but instead of complying the driver made the mistake of pressing his extremely loud horn and, without ceasing to press, edging the car ever closer to Carl's back wheel. The anger that possessed him spurred him on to power up the final fifty yards, as he'd be damned if he was going to pull over, and only on cresting the rise did he turn to glare at the lowlife cretins who had defiled his achievement with their stupid antics.

Rather than realising the error of their ways on seeing his livid and rather fearsome face, however, the driver accelerated slowly and on passing him the passenger hurled an opened beer can at his head, before they both howled with delight and sped off down the hill in the black BMW. Carl slowed to a halt and slumped panting over the bars, a few drops of the beer mingling with his sweat and reaching his lips. He spat in disgust before wiping his face on his sleeve and roaring at the tarmac. Just then he wanted to smash their faces to a pulp and stamp on their idiotic heads, and given the chance he knew that he'd have done it, but a vison of Janine, the prison psychologist, appeared before his mind's eye and he proceeded to take deep and deliberate breaths until he'd calmed down somewhat. He then dismounted and carefully leant the bike on a fence beside a cattle grid, before seating himself on the rough grass by the road and taking stock of the situation.

OK, so they'd spoilt his intrepid ascent, but what were the odds of such townie trash having coincided with him on that stretch of road? Ten thousand to one? God only knew what riffraff like them were doing so far away from their natural environment – the slums of Blackburn or suchlike, he guessed – and he shook his head in disbelief before looking up at the sparse, puffy clouds and wondering if the aforementioned God had sent them along to test him. Ha, yes, that might be it, because when you suffer extended stretches of solitary as he had done during the first few years of his sentence, you get to thinking about all sorts of things, including Him up there. After shifting his backside in order to cross his legs, he closed his eyes and breathed in slowly through his nose, before exhaling through his mouth and repeating the drill until he felt truly calm. He then forced himself to put the incident out of his mind and instead concentrate on the next part of the route which he'd memorised the night before; a long descent to Marshaw, followed by a left turn and straight on all the way to Scorton.

He pushed himself to his feet, walked over the cattle grid, remounted and began to freewheel down the hill, braking only when a car approached, occupied by an elderly couple who both smiled at him. *They* are the sort of folk you expect to meet out here, not those bloody arseholes, and while a joke's a joke, they'd gone way too far when they'd hurled the half-full can at him. It was lucky that he'd never see them again – for them and him alike – and as the lane rose onto the moors once more he gripped the bars and tried to ride them out of his mind.

By the time he passed the Scorton sign after an enjoyable descent he was looking forward to finding a shop and buying something more filling to eat than the paltry cereal bars, as he still had a long way to go and knew that the terrain would be challenging as far as Chipping. In the Spar shop he bought a homemade pie, a chocolate-filled pastry and a half-litre bottle of coke and he was casting around for a convenient bench when he saw the black BMW parked across the road in front of a telephone box. Beyond the cubicle was a single-storey pub with some picnic tables outside. He saw several civilised-looking people sitting there, but no-one who resembled the chavs who'd so blighted his ride, so he assumed they were inside, presumably going on with their drinking session.

Carl suddenly felt like he was back in the yard at the high-security nick where he'd played the hard man so foolishly for three or four years. There he'd always been on his guard, however relaxed he might have appeared as he strolled around with his cronies, and he found himself slipping into that apparently insouciant mode as he planned his strategy. There were no public benches within view, but further along the street he saw more picnic tables belonging to a café, so he stashed his victuals, got on his bike and rode past the pub, his face averted, before leaning the machine near another bike and taking a seat at the second table. The family group seated between him and the pub enabled him to keep his eye the doorway without fear of detection and after ordering a pot of tea and a scone he settled down to wait. He looked calm because he was. He had ceased to think and would allow his subconscious mind to dictate his actions. Something was going to happen, he knew that, but as he munched the crumbly scone and sipped his tea he felt incurious as to how the ensuing scene would unfold. As his mind processed the distance from the pub door to the car, and all the people within view, his hand extracted a ten pound note from his wallet and slid one end under the teapot.

He remained in this trancelike state for a while and only when he topped up his cup did a single, definite thought push through the haze; that he could just ride away and forget about the whole thing. He sniggered softly as he poured the milk and went on watching the pub door. No, he had to confront them and as words would carry no weight with such brainless scum his instincts alone would determine the outcome.

Just then loud voices emanated from the pub and he saw that their unwelcome presence had produced an altercation, as a slim, white-shirted man had emerged through the narrow door and was ordering them to leave, something they were clearly disinclined to do, judging by their jeers of derision. The outdoor customers looked on with concern, as did the people around him, while Carl almost whooped for joy before standing up and walking briskly down to the pub, glad that he'd chosen the type of cycling shoes that you can walk normally in. Once there he gently pushed the waiter aside and entered the pub, closing the door behind him.

About five minutes later he was back on his bike, heading up a steep hill which the flood of adrenaline enabled him to take in his stride. He hadn't planned to ride up this narrow lane, but in view of recent events he'd thought it wise to avoid the busier road towards Garstang. On reaching the top he noticed the blood seeping through the backs of his fingerless gloves for the first time and found himself laughing out loud, before curtailing his mirth as he passed a house. He wasn't out of the woods yet, and despite having politely asked the bemused waiter not to tell the police that he'd taken the lane, when he'd re-entered his pub to find the two thoroughly battered men it was anyone's guess what he might have done.

Speaking of woods, he found he was cycling through a rather dense one, so he decided to err on the side of caution and hide in it for a while. He left the lane and scampered through the undergrowth until he came to a stream. Sure enough, about ten minutes later when he was rinsing his gloves and soaking his swelling hands he heard the sound of a siren followed by what must have been a police car going at full pelt. Maybe the waiter had found the results of the cyclist's chastisement excessive and felt compelled to put the cops on his trail, and it was only then that Carl grasped the magnitude of his vengeful attack. Oh my God, he thought, if they catch me I'll be back inside and won't be coming out for a very long time. After a headbutt and a right hook both of the tall, slim lads had been practically KOed, so had it really been necessary to pummel them about the head until his arms felt like his legs had done on the Trough of Bowland? He'd then given them a kicking for good measure until one lay limp and the other squealed for mercy. Though their punishment might well dissuade them from embarking on another boozy road trip, Carl couldn't help thinking that he ought to have stopped when he'd broken the first lad's nose.

Suddenly exhausted by the day's exertions he found a flat bit of grass and lay down. After a while he dozed off, which was just as well, as when he awoke an hour later he heard a car and observed flashing lights through the trees. He decided to stay put for another hour and during that time he ate his lunch and debated whether or not he ought to give up cycling and find another hobby less likely to enflame his volatile temperament.

"Let's see if I make it home without them catching me first," he murmured, before stashing his yellow top in a pannier and putting on his red rain jacket. His gloves though wet were clean, so he pulled them onto his tender hands and made his way back to the lane. Due to his impetuous actions his ride back to Whalley turned into a real killer, as he felt compelled to stick to the hillier and less frequented lanes. The hours he'd spent poring over online maps served him well and when he finally rolled to a halt beside his car he had the satisfaction of seeing that he'd clocked up almost sixty miles. His legs felt like lead and he had to prise his stiffening hands from the bars, but he'd made it and looked forward to a long, hot bath.

4

"Ha, you must have really got the cycling bug," Mike said to him three days later at the probation office.

"Yes, I know it's a bit daft to wear the gloves all the time, but... well, I just like them," he said sheepishly as he flexed his still-bruised hands and examined the new track mitts he'd bought online and had sent by express delivery, along with a green cycling jacket and a white helmet, having consigned his incriminating gear to a bin bag which he'd taken to the local tip. He'd even thought about disposing of his precious bike, but it was a discreet colour and he doubted that anyone would have noticed the make, as when he rode away people were still unaware of his bloody rampage and the waiter had stepped inside to witness the carnage.

"So, tell me all about the rides you've done so far," said Mike, settling down to enjoy an hour of cycling chatter.

Carl described the tough five hundred miles he'd ridden on the mountain bike and Mike interjected anecdotes of his own from time to time. He chided him for not having mentioned his name at the bike shop, as he was sure that

Sandra would have knocked a bit off his bill if he had done so.

"Oh, I didn't like to, Mike. I'm not one for namedropping."

"So, how are you liking the new bike?"

"Oh, it's great. So much lighter."

"It's the wheels that make the most difference, you know, and if you get lighter tyres you'll go even faster," he said with enthusiasm. "Where have you been on it?"

Carl cleared his throat. "I've been driving to Gisburn and riding up the lanes north of there mostly."

"Ah, to Rathmell and Settle?"

"Yes, well, I didn't go into Settle as it's a big place, but I've been to Austwick and Clapham," he lied, as the bike hadn't moved from the garage since that action-packed day. "I've been to Malham and Grassington too," he added, both places even further from the scene of the crime.

"Oh, I envy you having all that free time!" He looked through the window at the cloudy sky. "I'd be out every day if I could."

"Does the traffic never bother you, Mike?"

"I try not to let it worry me and I stay off the main roads as much as I can."

"Me too. At first the cars scared me a bit, especially when they got too close, but I'm getting used to them now."

"Yes, you'll have the odd scare from time to time, but you mustn't let it bother you. If it was up to a lot of motorists they'd have cycling banned, so we have to stick up for ourselves. The more cyclists there are, the more they'll be forced to respect us. Since we started doing well at the

Olympics and in the Tour loads more folk have taken it up, which is good news. Cycling's the future, as people will see when petrol costs a fiver a litre," he said with a chuckle.

"When I get fitter I'm going to go touring," Carl said, as despite his unfortunate reversion to his violent past he was determined to draw a line under it and be more careful in future. Like Mike said, you couldn't let a minority of drivers put you off, and over the last three days he'd given much thought to other ways of castigating offenders without causing them bodily harm and risking a return to prison. Though he didn't regret having smashed up those two hooligans, especially when he recalled the beer can hitting his helmet, he knew that most future wrongdoers wouldn't deserve that sort of treatment. He also knew himself, however, and was aware that it wasn't in his nature to let miscreants off scot-free. During his later prison years he'd been forced to do so from time to time in order to secure his own release, but those incidents still rankled and as a free man he had a right to stand up for himself.

Thus it was that two parallel trains of thought developed in Carl's mind; how to get the most out of cycling and how to be prepared for the inevitable incidents that would occur on the road. By planning ahead he reasoned that he'd be less likely to commit another act of folly like the one in Scorton, and with this in mind his touring bike would carry extra accessories not found on any cycle touring checklist.

"I used to go touring before I was married," Mike said wistfully. "But now I prefer a lighter bike and faster rides. Besides, the wife plans our holidays and none of them involve cycling, worse luck. Will you camp out?"

"Oh, I don't think so. I think I'll stop at B&Bs so I don't have to carry so much stuff."

"That's true. Yes, I think touring will be good for you. I don't like to talk shop, but it's true that it's important for you to socialise a bit."

"That's right, and because of my past I don't really feel like making new friends around here."

"No, but…"

"I'm not one of those who want to own up to his sins, Mike. You know, all this bollocks about disclosure and making a clean breast of it."

"Ha, well, it works for some people, but not for others."

"I just want to eradicate that part of my life from my… well, my life, and start afresh. I might even move someday, but I don't like to sell the house. I think cycle touring might be the answer, if that's all right with you, that is."

"As long as you're back for our meetings you can go anywhere in Britain, and anywhere in the world from next year. Of all the long-term prisoners I see, you're the one who's adapting best to freedom, the best by far. Keep up the good work," he said, reaching over to pat Carl's gloved hand.

"I'll try."

Carl felt relieved when he left the building because he knew that his crime – for there was no other word for it – had been reported in the *Garstang Courier* and the western edition of the *Lancashire Evening Post*, but not in the East Lancashire papers, as he'd perused the press online before deleting his search history. It would be a long time before he frequented the roads within ten miles of Scorton again, if ever, which was a pity, but he looked forward to riding the northern routes he'd described to Mike and decided to drive to Gisburn right away.

After parking near the cattle market he headed off down the lane towards Bolton-by-Bowland, before taking a right onto a rough, deserted lane. Though stiff at first he soon got into his rhythm and felt stronger than ever after his prudent layoff. On the lanes he'd memorised he headed towards Wigglesworth and as he reached the top of a long drag he saw the first peaks of the Yorkshire Dales before him. He identified Ingleborough and Pen-y-Ghent from the maps and really liked the look of the limestone which began to succeed the darker Lancashire stone. He knew that the Dales stretched away many miles to the north and east and couldn't wait to explore the network of peaceful lanes. The road to Rathmell proved to be slightly busier and a white van passed him a little more quickly than he'd have liked, so as he focussed on the fells he mused about whether hiking mightn't be a better pastime for him. Up in the hills, off the beaten track, who or what could possibly endanger him? A flock of angry sheep? But though hiking gave him food for thought, when he swooped down to the flatland beyond Rathmell he knew that trudging up and down paths wasn't a patch on spinning along on a smooth, flat road or getting stuck into a really tough climb, knowing that an exhilarating descent would follow.

No, cycling it had to be, and as he turned off a mercifully brief stretch of main road onto another quiet lane he felt reassured by the resources he'd assembled – both on his bike and in his mind – to counter anyone who dared to invade his space while he cycled. Nine times out of ten he wouldn't catch them, of course, but if or when he did they'd surely lament having crossed this innocuous-looking rider! Carl knew more than most about delinquency and chastisement and in his mind the simple and irrevocable equation was *crime = punishment*. It was as straightforward as that, always had been and always would be. Now that he felt prepared he tried to banish such thoughts from his mind and simply enjoy the ride, but as he carefully crossed the main road and headed into Austwick he felt an absurd sense of disappointment that no vehicle had come within less than a yard of him. He shook his head and chuckled as he leant his bike against the wall of the village store. The Scorton affair was just too recent, he surmised, and granted a few eventless rides he'd soon put it behind him and cease to fret about such things.

After a tasty Cornish pasty, a couple of Eccles Cakes and a bottle of coke which he consumed on the bench outside the shop, he went back inside and got a coffee from the machine. It proved to be delicious and strong enough to make him wish to set off without delay, so he popped inside to say goodbye to the friendly lady shopkeeper and hit the road. Though planning to return by the same route, he soon conceived the strange notion of making a detour via the busy market town of Settle, and as he cycled along he asked himself what possessed him to desire to do such a thing. Was he simply looking for trouble by entering its busy streets, some of which were bound to be narrow? No, of course not, but it would be good to do a bit of urban cycling just for practice and to assuage his fears about having so many cars around him. Yes, although he'd avoided cycling in his own town he could do worse than get used to that type of riding, as on his projected cycle tours he was bound to have to traverse busy towns or even cities at some point. In this way he convinced himself to ride along a stretch of the A65 – also good practice – and enter the town by way of the railway station.

Once on the main street he turned left and pedalled along with the slow-moving cars, none of which tried to pass him, so when he reached a petrol station on the edge of town he crossed the road and headed back. Just before the market square the road narrowed considerably and as it widened a car eased past a tad too closely, but no, he was a competent driver and hadn't endangered him at all. So far, so good, he thought as he turned sharp left and headed up an ever-steepening street. As he puffed and panted up a narrow stretch, he stayed over to the left to see if the driver behind him would get impatient, squeeze past and thus incur his wrath, but no, the car remained ten yards behind him until he turned right and freewheeled until the street rose again and he realised that he was using energy that might be better spent on the open road.

Settle was clearly a prosperous place, he reflected, and the inhabitants far too civilised to upset a cyclist, so once back on the main street he knew he ought to give the residents a tick of approval and head back to Gisburn, but something made him cycle through the town once more, this time riding further away from the kerb than he really needed to and weaving slightly as if exhausted. This tactic simply made the drivers give him an even wider berth, so after the petrol station he turned left down a residential street, intending to make his way back to the train station.

He cycled down the street in a carefree way, pleased by his experiment and feeling one step closer to a more harmonious relationship with motorised road users but, as luck would have it, just as he was approaching the station a small Citroen pulled quickly out of a driveway, causing him to brake sharply. Rather than shouting or waving his fist, however, Carl looked down at the road, accelerated smoothly and pedalled on as if nothing had happened. At the junction with Station Road he hoped the car would turn left into town rather than right and out of his reach, so when the left indicator flashed he lowered his head and grinned. He didn't lug around his extra equipment for nothing, after all, and if the driver was off to do an errand he would probably get the chance to try out one of his punishment methods.

The beauty of his new approach was that it didn't matter how old or frail the driver was, as he only intended to hit his or her pocket. In his panniers he possessed the means to extract 'fines' ranging from a few pounds to several thousand, and though he wouldn't benefit from the money, they'd think twice before they abused another rider. Or would they? he pondered as the car turned towards the town square, because as things stood he doubted if the driver had even realised that only Carl's reflexes had saved him from skidding or even taking a tumble. Until then he hadn't thought about this eventuality, as he'd envisioned rather closer shaves which the driver couldn't help being aware of, so as he stalked the car he chose the method he would use, given the chance, as however minor the offence he was about to commit, he daren't risk detection.

With this in mind he was glad when the driver – a man and probably quite elderly – turned right, as had he parked in the square Carl would have had to substitute his chosen 'fixed penalty' for another more discreet one, but when he saw the car pull into a fortuitous parking space opposite a shop he rode on by, his head down and chuckling to himself. A hundred yards along the street he dismounted and fiddled with his bike until he saw the tweedy old chap lock the car and stroll back towards the town centre. The silly sod would have done better to walk from home, Carl thought, as his car journey had been unnecessary and was about to cost him. He opened the left-hand pannier bag and found the spray can, but when he reflected on the levity of the man's offence – he'd only made Carl brake hard, after all – he relented and rooted for the permanent marker instead. This would cause more dismay and inconvenience than cost, but he didn't wish to be too harsh on the old duffer, and besides, the shop had windows.

Despite the clement weather he put on his rain jacket – a blue one – and stretched a matching lycra cover over his helmet, before wheeling his bike back towards the car and leaning it against the stone wall. While he fiddled with the gears he looked up and down the street and over at the shop, before unsheathing his thick black marker and writing 'I KILL CYCLISTS' in large, firm letters stretching from the front to rear wings, before sliding the marker into his rear pocket, walking his bike down the pavement, and remounting once clear of the shop. He tried his best to keep a straight face as he cycled past the police station, but once he was coasting down the hill out of town he laughed so heartily that he almost forgot to stop to take off his blue items of clothing. This he did when he paused to admire the fast-flowing River Ribble, but he saw no reason to jettison anything more than the marker pen, as he was sure that no-one had seen him.

On the flat road to Rathmell he powered along and even managed to get up the drag to the village without resorting to the small chainring. His mischievous act appeared to have given him wings and he was in an excellent mood all the way back to Gisburn, his twin desires having been well satisfied. He'd enjoyed the ride *and* struck a blow, albeit a symbolic one, for cyclists' rights. He knew it had been little more than a rehearsal for greater things to come, but he felt chuffed about the way he'd kept his cool and he looked forward to employing his armoury more effectively in future, if, and only if, motorists didn't respect him.

He thought it a shame that he didn't have any friends he could share his plans and exploits with – most of his prison buddies would have lapped it up – but on the whole he was happy to operate alone. Yes, he really was a lone wolf in lycra!

5

It rained on and off for the next fortnight, but this didn't deter Carl from getting out on his bike most days. He began to drive to the village of Sawley where, if he arrived early enough, he could park next to the river and unwind on the grass beside it after his ride, feeding himself and the ducks that soon got to know him well enough to eat crumbled up cereal bars out of his hand. He found the river soothing after his exertions which now took him as far afield as Ingleton, Ribblehead and Kettlewell, but not even on the busy, narrow road to this latter destination had the motorists bothered him, despite going on a Sunday when it was busier than ever. As he rode along he sometimes thought fondly of his daring bit of vandalism in Settle, but on the whole he was glad that he could concentrate on his cycling and feel himself getting stronger as each week passed. It would soon be time to embark on a tour, but before that he had set himself the challenge of riding to Hawes by way of Kettlewell and returning via Ribblehead, a hilly eighty-mile slog from Sawley.

He chose a warm, sunny day in early June on which to do this epic ride and had rested the day before when he had seen Mike again.

"Ha, the browner and slimmer you get, the more jealous I feel," he'd said no sooner had Carl walked into the room. "I think you're even getting a bit bow-legged, the unmistakable sign of a true cyclist."

Carl grinned, patted his growing thighs and sat down. "Are you getting out at the weekends?"

"Yes, I'm allowed out all day Sunday, but only for a couple of hours on Saturday as we have to go shopping and stuff. I get out at least two evening too, so I'm managing almost two hundred miles most weeks," he said, before frowning briefly as he turned to the computer screen.

"What's up?"

"Oh, I've just remembered that we're going to Majorca for ten days soon."

"Is that a bad thing?"

"Well, no, it's our main holiday and I'll be glad to get away from here for a while, but… well, I won't be able to do any cycling so I'll lose a bit of fitness."

"You could hire a bike for a few days."

"Oh, I did once, but she was grumpy about it. No, I'll just have to try to enjoy myself in the usual way, though I get bored silly on the beach."

"I suppose I'm lucky to be able to do whatever I want, but I do sort of miss female company."

"Have you not… you know, had a bit of a fling since you got out?" Mike asked quietly.

"Haven't had the opportunity."

"Mm, I'm sure if you went out on a Saturday night you'd find some bird who'd be up for a bit of fun, especially now that you're looking so fit." He cleared his throat. "I know it's none of my business, but it's just an idea."

"Oh, I've thought about it, but it's not my scene anymore. I don't think I could stand it in a noisy pub. I'd want to leave straight away. No, maybe when I start touring I'll meet a more… wholesome woman who I might get on with," he said, before telling him about his planned ride to Hawes.

"Ah, over Fleet Moss! That's a toughie, but it's a lovely ride up that valley, then back over Ribblehead. You know, I've a good mind to call in sick and come with you."

"Do it. We could meet at Sawley."

Mike sucked in air through his teeth. "Oh, I'd better not. If anyone saw me I could lose my job."

"What, just for sneaking a day off?"

"Well, er… and being out with you."

"Oh, yes, I forgot I was still a social leper," he said mildly.

"No, but rules are rules, and mine are strict. Like I said before, you could join the club and come out with us on Sundays."

"Thanks, but I don't know. I can't see myself riding in a group."

"Try it one day and see if you like it."

"We'll see. Is there anything else we have to talk about today?"

"Like what?"

"Well, probation stuff."

"Not unless you want to." He smiled. "I already know what I'm going to write. Is anything bothering you?"

"No, not at all."

"Good. Did you get some lighter tyres?"

"No, I'll wear out the ones I've got first."

"Well…" Mike began, and they spent the rest of their allotted time talking tyres, wheels, gears and brakes.

The following morning Carl drove into Sawley at half past eight with feelings of both enthusiasm and trepidation. It was going to be a tough ride and he mustn't set off too fast, as he hoped to get round without becoming completely exhausted, because when he did his first five or six-day cycle tour at the end of the month he planned to ride that sort of distance every day. With this in mind he tackled the long drag towards Wigglesworth in a low gear and rode on through Hellifield, Winterburn and Cracoe well within his limits. On the Kettlewell road the traffic annoyed him a bit, but it had been so long since anyone had invaded his space that he was able to switch off, more or less, and enjoy the wonderful Wharfedale scenery. As the café at Kettlewell was quiet he decided to stop for a pot of tea and a bacon butty before riding on to Buckden, where he would turn left onto the reputedly beautiful lane through Yockenthwaite and on to the challenging Fleet Moss climb.

It felt so nice sitting in the sun at the Cottage Tearoom that he had half a mind to laze about there for a while and head back via Halton Gill, an isolated hamlet he also wished to visit, but no, he'd set himself the goal of getting to Hawes and he couldn't chicken out now. After asking the friendly owner to refill his empty water bottle he paid the bill and pottered away through the quaint village, taking it easy on the flattish road to Buckden and up the gentle slopes following the River Wharfe until the lane veered north and the climb proper began. It was wild and desolate up there and when he heard a car approaching he pulled over into a passing place, as he didn't wish any noisy, smelly vehicle to spoil his feeling of isolation for longer than it had too. The lady passenger thanked him as they passed and Carl felt serene and happy. When he rumbled over a cattle grid he remembered the Trough of Bowland, but his thoughts soon turned back to the present as he changed into a lower gear and braced himself for the final stretch to the summit. The climb was long but more gradual than he'd expected and at the top he was rewarded by a wonderfully clear view of the hills beyond Wensleydale.

After drinking in the scenery for a few minutes he swooped down a really steep bit before the gradient lessened and by touching his brakes from time to time he was able to enjoy the descent without ever feeling out of control. He was looking forward to getting his first view of Hawes when, on passing a farm, a large tractor pulled out right in front of him. Carl sat back over the saddle and slammed on both brakes, but his only escape was the narrow space between the huge rear wheel and the wall of a farm building, so he aimed at the gap and finally juddered to a halt alongside the driver, who looked over in surprise, before shrugging and pressing his foot to the floor, enveloping the petrified Carl in noxious fumes.

So, once more he found himself slumped over the handlebars gasping for breath, this time due to sheer fright rather than exertion. He couldn't have yelled at the driver if he'd wanted to, but when he finally looked up he was glad he hadn't. Let him drive merrily away, he thought, because the fat, crimson bastard will soon be getting what's coming to him and the less clearly he's seen me the better. The next time he pulls out of his farmyard, whenever that might be, he'll be looking a damn sight more carefully than he just did. He glanced around to check that no-one else had witnessed the scene, before riding slowly away, confident that the farmer wouldn't be going too far from home.

As he freewheeled along, sucking in the warm air in an effort to calm himself, he attempted to settle on a fitting punishment for the farmer's almost life-threatening deed, but try as he might he couldn't think altogether rationally after such a close call. It did occur to him that no matter how much damage he inflicted on the tractor, the great bumpkin's insurance would probably pay for most of it, so when he saw him up ahead, shutting a gate behind him, he knew that the man himself would bear the brunt of his anger. He'd looked like a big chap, however, and was probably as strong as an ox, so an element of surprise would be advisable.

As luck would have it there was an old building before the gate and during the last hundred yards of his approach he remained out of sight, so he pulled up alongside it, leant his bike on the wall, and peered around the corner of the rough stone structure. There he was, attaching some sort of machinery to the tractor, his fat arse sticking out of his jeans, so Carl seized the moment and vaulted the gate. The soft thud of his feet hitting the grass caused the farmer to begin to turn his head, but before he could meet Carl's blazing eyes he had struck him on the back of the neck with all his might, sending him senseless to the ground. Carl looked up and down the deserted road before crouching to inspect the damage. Blood was seeping through his scraggly grey hair and at first Carl couldn't recall having grasped the large stone that he'd hit him with, before realising that he'd snatched it from the wall beside the gate.

Alarmed but still vigilant, he dragged the gate open and looked up and down the road before wheeling his bike into the field and concealing it behind the building. The man hadn't moved and it was with some anxiety that Carl knelt down beside him and put his ear to the man's open mouth. He was breathing, thank God, and would soon come round, so after an especially thorough recce of the road he wheeled his bike out, pulled the gate closed behind him, and accelerated away, keen to reach the village of Gayle where he knew he could leave the Hawes road. Fortunately no cars passed him before he took a left turn and began to breathe more easily. He'd have to give Hawes a miss, worse luck, as he'd been looking forward to seeing it, but now it was in his best interests to get up to Ribblehead and far away from the scene.

So much for a relaxed ride, he thought as he powered up the gradual incline after joining the main road, but though he was working hard he tried not to look overly stressed as the sweat ran down his face. There were plenty of cars around now, but he doubted that the police would be on his case, as the farmer was probably still sleeping off his rather harsh punishment. He sniggered as he slogged up the last stretch because the ignorant wretch had got no less than he deserved. Cyclists were killed every day due to actions such as his and the culprits almost always got off with a fine and maybe a suspended sentence. In court it was usually their word against the dead cyclist's silence, so they could say the victim had been riding recklessly, not paying attention, or whatever they bloody well wanted to. That damn yokel would remember the day when he sat in his cabin and shrugged after almost causing a man's death, so Carl hoped that his recovery would be slow, painful and thought-provoking.

As he coasted down the smooth road towards Ribblehead Viaduct he hoped to grab a drink and a bite to eat at the butty van Mike had told him about, but just as the famous railway structure came into view Carl was dismayed to hear and *feel* two motorbikes whizz past him at an astonishing speed. He emitted a long and audible sigh. Oh, would his day's trials never end? One of the speed merchants had come within less than a yard of him at something approaching a hundred miles an hour and he couldn't be allowed to get away with it. Carl gripped the ends of his bars and immediately realised which punitive measure he would be taking within a few minutes. It bothered him not a jot whether they were near their bikes or not, as just then he was feeling as invincible as he used to during his early years in the nick. It would be handy if there were no more people about, of course, but Carl was set on trying out a tool which had cost him considerable work to perfect and he knew that now was the time to use it.

As he rolled to a halt fifty yards shy of the butty van, there they were, taking off their helmets to reveal youngish, mindless faces still glowing from their thrilling exploits which, Carl thought with scorn, were achieved by twisting their right hands a few centimetres now and then. The twerps were gabbling about something or other, so Carl bided his time by inspecting his bike and giving the right-hand bar end a little twist, just like they did, but with a different intention in mind. They'd parked up about twenty yards from the van behind two parked cars, so when they went in search of sustenance after their exertions it was child's play to wheel his bike towards the van, casually lean it on a car, extract the small, sharpened screwdriver which he'd glued into the bar end plug, and plunge it quickly into all four of the motorbikes' tyres, before pushing it back into place. The sound of the van's generator blotted out the delicious hissing sound and Carl was tempted to join them for a cuppa, but the bikers weren't as weedy as the Scorton scum had been, so he thought it best to go on his way before they cottoned on to their stranded state.

Despite his best intentions, this ride was turning into a taxing one, mainly due to having so little time to rest. Down the valley in Horton-in-Ribblesdale there was a café, but he decided to press on to Settle and buy food and drink at the petrol station. By the time he reached the car at Sawley he felt like Tour de France riders looked after a gruelling mountain stage, but at least all they had to worry about was riding their bikes. Yes, it had been a day to remember, and although he'd have to give those roads a miss for the rest of the summer he felt, as he relaxed in a hot bath, that it had all been worthwhile. Not only had those three people got their comeuppance, but all the folk who heard about the cyclist's revenge would perhaps treat riders with more respect from then on, lest they receive the same kind of treatment. That seemed like a logical enough argument to Carl, as he closed his eyes and plunged his head underwater.

6

People didn't only hear about the cyclist's revenge, but they also read about it, and not just in the *Westmorland Gazette*, but also briefly in the national press, as the farmer's life had been on the line for a few days until they'd operated on him and slowly released him from an induced coma. Carl followed the news closely online, always deleting the search immediately, and he was doubly relieved when the man came to and didn't remember much about what had happened. He'd been attaching a muck-spreader to his tractor when someone had walloped him on the head, was all he said, so unless the cops had told him to hold back information, Carl was in the clear once again. All the same, he was glad that Mike had flown off to Majorca on the day after the eventful ride and that his next probation meeting was a brief one with a smiling middle-aged woman who thought it lovely that he'd taken up cycling and splendid that he was keeping his nose clean.

He didn't go out for a week after the Hawes ride, as just like after the Scorton affair he preferred to lay low and muse on the non-cycling aspects of his outing, which caused him occasional pangs of guilt. He spent a long time online, reading about hiking, golf, foreign travel and other possible substitutes for cycling, but it was no good, he was hooked on the sport and he – and the drivers he might chance to meet – would have to take the rough with the smooth. In view of the fact that two excellent cycling zones were out of bounds for the time being, he decided to bring forward his first tour and explore a new area right away. He needed a change of scene and thought that south-west Scotland would be a fine, quiet place in which to get to grips with the logistics of day to day travel.

So it was that on a Thursday afternoon he drove up the M6 as far as Gretna Green, before heading west to the pleasant town of Castle Douglas where he'd already booked into a modest hotel with private parking for the night. As he completed the last leg along the A75 he felt a great sense of anticipation, as this was the first time since his father's funeral that he'd be mingling with people he didn't know. At the post-crematorium get-together, which he'd felt obliged to organise for his dad's considerable number of friends and acquaintances, he'd felt uncomfortable throughout, because he knew that they knew about his unwholesome past. Although most of them had been clearly impressed by his tailor-made suit, good manners and sobriety, it had been a taxing few hours and he'd felt liberated when it was finally over.

This trip wouldn't be like that. The hotel staff and other guests wouldn't know him from Adam, and just like when he'd popped into shops and cafés during his rides, they'd only see the agreeable, healthy man he wished to become.

The Castle Douglas hotel was the only one he'd booked, because he'd seen online that there were plenty of vacancies in Dumfries and Galloway. Better to take each day as it came, and he didn't rule out the option of staying in one place for two or more nights if the atmosphere were convivial enough. His dream of meeting the ideal woman on his travels persisted and he imagined first seeing her over breakfast or during an evening stroll, in which case he'd be loath to pedal away without giving their fortuitous encounter a chance to blossom into something special. He liked the way educated Scottish women spoke – on TV, for he'd never met any – and he could easily see himself relocating to a pretty highland or lowland village and starting afresh with his fine wee lassie! The kind of women he'd consorted with before being locked up were to be avoided at all costs, of course, but as he wouldn't be entering any pubs if he could help it, he thought there was little likelihood of meeting any of those.

When he sauntered into the hotel reception he looked every inch the reputable, rather affluent traveller in his discrete but top quality casual clothes. The young foreign woman greeted him with respect, before confirming his booking and showing him to his large second-floor room. The firm double bed met with his approval and he requested a table for dinner at seven. Sure that his bike would be safe in the car, he decided not to reveal he was a cyclist until the following morning, when he would drive to the public carpark and set off on his travels. Or would he? Maybe not if this evening he got chatting to his hypothetical soulmate – a slim brunette with lovely brown eyes and an endearing smile, perchance – as in that case the bike might remain in the car while he spent the week wining and dining her after halcyon days of strolling, sightseeing and catering to her every whim.

He chuckled into the mirror as he parted his damp hair, before shaving for the second time that day and dressing for dinner. He chose a blue shirt, a pair of beige chinos and his expensive new brogues from his small 'civilian' clothing suitcase, and after putting on his thousand pound Alpina watch he made his way to the dining room. None of the people present were of interest – two couples, a young family, and two men seated alone – but after ordering he remained hopeful that someone more alluring might put in an appearance. This didn't occur and he realised that it had been wishful thinking to have expected to happen upon *any* single women in the dining room, let alone one who met his criteria. He decided to take coffee in the lounge bar, but on beholding a similarly uninspiring scene he felt he had no choice but to enter the adjacent public bar and try his luck there.

Apart from the do after the funeral he hadn't entered anything remotely resembling a pub since his release, with the exception of his brief and bloody foray into the one at Scorton. As he no longer touched a drop of booze he saw no reason to visit them, and besides, pubs had been the backdrop to many unpleasant incidents in his younger days, as no matter how well he'd behaved, more often than not someone ended up picking a fight with him. Neither he nor his erstwhile pals could explain it, but he seemed to be a magnet for aggro and it had been lucky for him that his drinking and drug taking hadn't blunted his reflexes too badly and he'd normally come out on top in these clashes, often due to his rejection of the rules of gentlemanly fisticuffs. A couple of his uglier encounters crossed his mind as he entered the busy pub – both involving glassware – but he smiled pleasantly as he approached the bar and ordered an alcohol-free beer from the portly bartender. He found a vacant stool where the bar met the wall and from there he was able to mind his own business and keep his eyes peeled for any promising 'talent'.

Being a Thursday evening there was a pre-weekend feel to the place and a group of young men were knocking back pints with gusto, while the older patrons were mostly engaged in conversations that Carl could scarcely understand. He was beginning to feel a bit fed up when two women of about thirty arrived and settled themselves at a table, before the taller one went up to the bar and ordered two of those alcopop drinks that had barely existed when Carl had been a man about town. Both of the girls were brunettes and the shorter, curvaceous one quite pretty, and though he sensed that neither was very classy he glanced over from time to time and eventually made eye contact with the taller one, who wasn't *too* bad looking and had a pleasant though rather vacant face. When he ordered another beer he poured the insipid stuff into a glass and pushed the blue-labelled bottle away, because if or when he approached the girls he didn't wish them to think him a tedious teetotaller.

He could have done with a real drink to dispel the slight inhibitions he felt about making such a bold move, but what the hell, he was far from home and all they could do was make him feel unwelcome, upon which he'd make a dignified exit and go to get some sleep. He was out of practice and felt that he had to test himself in a situation like this, because there was more to life than cycling up hill and down dale, so he smoothed his hair, picked up his glass and made his way across to them.

"Hi, do you mind if I join you for a while," he said, nodding towards the spare chair.

"Gay ahead," the tall one said, or that's how it sounded.

He sat down and beamed at them both. "I'm away from home and was feeling a bit bored," he said with a shrug.

"You a traveller?" said the buxom one who Carl now saw wore way too much makeup.

"Yes, I'm travelling."

She giggled. "Nay, a salesman or summat."

"Oh, no, I'm on holiday. A cycling tour, actually."

This confession left them both a bit nonplussed, so Carl asked them if they knew the Galloway Forest Park.

"I've been to Newton Stewart... oh, shite, here's your Callum," said the tall one.

"Aye, well, it's been nice chatting to you," said the other, casting an anxious glance at the strapping chap who'd just joined the group of young men.

Carl weighed him up and couldn't resist asking them if they were leaving.

"No, well, it's just that..."

At that moment the new arrival looked over, scrunched up his eyes, and strode over to the table. He was about thirty too, and sported elaborate tattoos on his muscular arms, bare to the shoulders as he was wearing a crass skin-tight vest. He reminded Carl of the Scorton chavs a bit, but if push came to shove this one wouldn't go down so easily.

"Who's the old fella, Fiona?" he asked, before staring daggers at Carl, who smiled politely up at him.

"Just a chap having a chat with us," she said a trifle anxiously.

"From out of town," said her friend. "Are you at the hotel?" she asked Carl.

"Yes, just for the night. I'm off tomo–"

"Fucking English too."

"That's right. I'm Carl," he said as he stood up and held out his hand.

Ignoring Carl's gracious greeting, he said something unintelligible to his girlfriend, but the gist was that she'd better get shut of the interloper and quick. After giving Carl a parting glare, he rejoined his ebullient pals and stood with his back to the trio, still without a drink. Carl knew that the tattooed tough guy was giving him a chance to beat a tactical retreat without losing face, but try as he might to stand up, he found himself glued to the chair.

"He didn't seem very friendly," he said with an innocent grin.

"No, he's a jealous fella," said the flustered Fiona with a frown.

"It might be best if you go back up to the bar, er…"

"Oh, gosh, I forgot to introduce myself. I'm Carl."

"Helen."

"Fiona."

Carl narrowed his eyes and chuckled. "I commit *faux pas* like that now and then, me having been away for so long."

"Faux what?" Fiona asked.

"Where were you?"

"In prison, for sixteen years. They finally let me out a few months ago, under certain conditions."

"What conditions?" Fiona asked, no longer glancing anxiously at her bloke.

"Ha, that I don't murder anyone else."

"You're kidding," said Helen, though she knew he wasn't, not now that she'd had a good look at those rather sinister blue eyes of his.

Carl glanced over at the lads and gently pressed each of the knuckles of his right hand in turn. "No, I'm not." He smiled. "I'll tell you what though. When you've stabbed someone to death you certainly get a taste for it."

The girls just looked at him goggle-eyed. This was better than EastEnders.

He chuckled and slapped his thighs. "No doubt I'll kill again one day, but hopefully not today, as I'm looking forward to my cycle tour. So what's Newton Stewart like, Helen?"

She gulped. "All right. So, why did you… er, stab someone?"

Just then Fiona's boyfriend turned to glance over. On seeing the tanned, stocky Sassenach still seated with his beloved he puffed out his cheeks, expelled the air and glanced up at the ceiling, before shaking his head and beginning to pick his way through the ever-increasing throng. Fiona jumped up, met him half way, and steered him towards the bar.

Carl yawned long and loud. "Excuse me, Helen. I think it's my bedtime. It's been a pleasure to meet you both. Goodnight."

"G'night."

He took a long, hard look at the boyfriend's back –Fiona was plying him with drink and chattering in his ear – and left the bar, before entering the hotel and going up to his room. Referring to his past had been a handy way of extricating himself from a scrap, as he knew that he couldn't have retreated meekly, but he didn't feel altogether happy about having played his trump card in this way. He had sworn to himself never to mention any of his crimes to anyone, let alone the most serious of them all, and though he'd probably never see those folk again it bugged him that by breakfast time some of the people around him might have heard the news. As he slipped between the fresh-smelling sheets he promised himself that he wouldn't enter any more pubs on the trip, as he always had such damn bad luck in those places.

7

His first thought on waking up at half past six was of the muscly prat who'd interrupted his first attempt to chat up – or at least chat to – some women. To alter his train of thought he took his map with him to the toilet and was soon able to focus on the day ahead, when he intended to cycle to Portpatrick by way of Newton Stewart, avoiding the main roads whenever possible. He was first in to breakfast and immediately knew that the young waitress had heard nothing about last night's revelation, so he settled down to enjoy his bacon and eggs, before booking a hotel on his phone while he sipped his second cup of coffee.

When he left the hotel at eight the traffic was light, but by the time he'd driven to the public carpark, taken out his bike, finished packing his panniers and divested himself of the clothing he was wearing over his cycling gear, the rush hour had begun. It wasn't much of a rush hour, so he set off right away and it was while waiting at a set of traffic lights that he glanced over and saw the tattooed brute of the night before. In his helmet and sunglasses Carl didn't think the oaf would recognise him, but he looked down anyway and when the small plumber's van crossed the junction into slow-moving traffic he found himself following, despite the fact that he ought to have turned left.

Is it fate that has thrown us together once more? Carl thought as he followed, three cars behind. Am I destined to punish him for trying to humiliate me last night? He wasn't sure, but he decided to stay on his tail for as long as he could anyway, in case fate gave him the opportunity to leave some kind of memento on the young tradesman's vehicle. Carl had just the thing in his new saddlebag, but doubted that circumstances would prevail neatly enough to allow him to use it, so it might just have to be a couple of jabs in the tyres with his trusty tool, if that, for he couldn't risk jeopardising his trip due to a non-cycling-related grudge.

When his prey turned onto a leafy suburban street Carl hung back a hundred yards and when the van stopped, so did he. As he adjusted his bags he saw the man open the back doors of the van and take out a tool bag, before approaching a house and being admitted. Tradesmen are apt to forget things, so Carl rode past and coasted down the street, biding his time and mentally rehearsing his forthcoming action, before stopping to prepare his materials. About fifteen minutes later he rode back, checked there was no-one around and positioned himself on the street side of the newish van, before folding a postcard into a triangular shape and popping it onto the roof. He then pulled the slim can from under his jacket, screwed off the top, and poured some of the liquid along his side of the van, paying special attention to the garish lettering. He then leant its bottom end on the postcard and observed the initial glugs, before cycling briskly back towards the main road, chuckling softly to himself.

It wasn't long before he was on the flat A713 which he soon left to take a B-road to Glenlochar and Laurieston, after which he would head along a minor road to the Gatehouse of Fleet. It proved to be a lovely, quiet route, especially the latter part, and as he rode along, the sun popping out from time to time, he soon ceased to think about his daring act of sabotage. The heavy-duty paint stripper would soon have done its worst, and when the great lummox saw the postcard of the hotel he would probably put two and two together and realise that the murderer had decided to spare his life and instead gain his revenge in this ingenious way. That's how Carl saw it anyway, as a perfectly reasonable reaction to the young man's hostile behaviour, so as he cycled through the stunning moorland scenery with the road to himself, he felt that all was well with the world.

After halting to eat a snack at the Gatehouse of Fleet – a picturesque little village – he headed north on a B-road which gradually curved round to the west and brought him out on the A75, the main road to Stranraer which he had to endure for a few miles until he reached Newton Stewart. With almost half of his day's ride covered, he visited a bakery and took his provisions to a bench by the River Cree where the slow-moving water soothed his mind. Reflecting on his abortive attempt to socialise the night before, he concluded that it wasn't worth the bother. He was destined to be a loner from now on, which suited him most of the time, so he would put those crazy ideas about meeting a soulmate out of his mind and just enjoy the journey.

Happy with his decision, he was soon back on the bike and by travelling via Challoch, Balminnoch and Whitecairn he was able to reach Glenluce without going on the dratted trunk road. The scenery – a mixture of moorland, pastureland and forests – was wonderful and the roads so deserted that it occurred to him that he could do worse than sell up and buy a house in the area. Not in Castle Douglas, of course, as there he might have a furious plumber to contend with, but maybe in or near Newton Stewart, from where roads headed off in all directions. As he coasted down a hill he reminded himself that the Scorton and Hawes areas were already out of bounds and there would be little point moving to good cycling country only to have those blasted motorists cause him to retaliate and thus gradually reduce his stomping ground until there was nowhere safe to ride.

He could rent a place, of course, and move on every year or so, but the absurdity of these reflections made him slow to a halt on the next rise and lean the bike against a wall. A moment of particular lucidity made him realise that in some ways he was his own worst enemy. Other cyclists, like Mike, managed to control their anger and never retaliated when a driver endangered them, or only by having recourse to the law, assuming they were able to memorise the culprit's registration number. He had read that the police were gradually becoming more sympathetic to the plight of cyclists and were now pursuing and prosecuting dangerous drivers more scrupulously than before. Though he'd never seen eye to eye with the cops in his younger days, he realised that a sensible citizen would never take the law into his own hands as he had got into the habit of doing.

As a first step towards this optimistic new outlook he unbuckled his panniers and rooted around inside them. He extracted the can of black spray paint and threw it over the wall, followed by his trusty marker pen and a cylinder of thick foam which he'd intended to shove up some reprobate's exhaust pipe, though he wasn't sure how effective that might be. He also chucked away a few large ball bearings that he'd put in on a whim, but hesitated when it came to a small tinsmith's hammer which he'd thought might be handy for smashing car windows. No, he'd hang onto that and put it back with his dad's other tools, and as for his handlebar-end tyre stabber, well, it was just too neat an article to dispense with right away. He'd keep that for now, as it gave him a warm feeling inside when he gripped that part of the bar and it wouldn't do to be completely defenceless. The paint stripper had already been jettisoned, to good effect, so as well as helping him to avoid further temptation, this clear-out would lighten his load by a couple of pounds, and every touring cyclist worth his salt avoids excess weight.

After Glenluce he had no choice but to join the A75 for a mile or so and a busy, narrow stretch it proved to be, with no sanctuary for cyclists beyond the white line. A slow lorry had caused a convoy to build up behind it, so for the whole mile Carl was being passed by vehicles, none of which came too close. Even so, he decided to get into the habit of looking at number plates as each car came by so that if or when someone cut him up he could call the police and see if they really did give a damn about cyclists' rights. On turning left onto a much quieter B-road towards Portpatrick he felt really pleased about this new strategy, though in the back of his mind there lurked another less lawful use he could make of the memorisation of number plates. He knew that Gary, who he'd shared a cell with for a few months, was well in with certain coppers in Manchester, but no, that was no way to think, especially after just resolving to try to cease his reprisals.

He shook his head and pedalled on along the straight, flat road. He still had a long way to go and he strove to put all negative thoughts out of his mind. He'd promised himself to turn over a new leaf, so that was quite enough of speculating on the same damn subject. Had any driver bothered him so far in Scotland? No, they hadn't. If anything they were even more respectful than most English motorists, so it was time to turn off that scratched record inside his head and get on with the business of becoming a hardened cycle tourist.

Entering the hotel reception in Portpatrick was a different experience to his arrival at the one in Castle Douglas. Instead of breezing in like an urbane man of leisure, he trudged up to the counter, sweaty and knackered after his seventy-odd mile ride. It was a stylish, modern hotel down by the harbour and he felt out of place in his cycling togs until the cheerful lady who attended him put him at his ease by asking him about his day's journey. It transpired that quite a few cyclists and walkers stayed there, so the sedentary appearance of the other guests he saw made him feel rather proud of his day's work. While they'd been dabbing at the accelerator he'd been turning the pedals, and besides, once he'd stowed away his bike, showered and changed into his casual clothes he'd no longer look so conspicuous.

As the evening was quite balmy, rather than eating in the dining room or at another restaurant, he bought fish and chips from a van and ate them down by the harbour, before strolling along to stretch his legs and sitting down at a different bench. As he watched the people go by he felt far happier than he had the previous night in that naff pub with all those boozers around him. It occurred to him that he might like to try cycle-camping, as although it would mean lugging a lot more stuff around, it would give him more autonomy and tranquillity. What was the use of other folk anyway? All they did was cause him grief and although he enjoyed a brief chat now and then, he really did prefer his own company. Maybe having been inside for so long had made him unsociable, or even badly adapted to normal life but, barring his regrettable scrapes, he'd enjoyed himself well enough since returning to the family home. He scarcely saw anyone when he was there, so why go looking for company on his travels? Yes, a tent might be just the thing, though that night he was more than happy to slip into his comfortable bed, where he slept solidly for nine hours.

8

The next morning he went down to breakfast in his cycling clothes with his map under his arm. He'd woken up in an excellent mood, partly due to his good resolutions of the previous day, and he felt like a chat before setting off to explore the area to the north and south of Portpatrick, as he'd realised that if he rode seventy or eighty miles in a straight line every day he'd have soon covered the whole region and would find himself back in Castle Douglas, where he intended to chuck the bike into the car and make a quick getaway, just in case. At breakfast he hoped that his lycra gear might inspire someone to ask him where he was heading, and he was in luck, because a plump woman at the next table did inquire and he ended up chatting to her and her husband on and off throughout the meal. They were impressed that he cycled so far and though he belittled his modest achievements, when he finally made tracks he felt really good about himself, his chosen hobby, and the future that could be his if only he could learn to control his temper and turn the other cheek, or at least tone down his response.

So far the only truly dangerous incident had been caused by the tractor near Hawes and he'd ended up almost killing the man. A stern ticking off might have been more appropriate, because deep down he knew that the farmer hadn't done it on purpose. As he pottered along the quiet lanes of the Rhins of Galloway peninsula, rarely encountering another vehicle, he enjoyed the pastoral scenery and occasional glimpses of the Irish coast and felt that he really was close to turning over a new leaf. Drivers were unlikely to bother him in that remote spot, but when he took the main road towards Girvan the following day he vowed to be on his best behaviour. The law of averages made it highly likely that at some point during the two hundred plus miles he had yet to cover someone would endanger him in some way. That would be the test. Avowals were one thing, but reality quite another, and if he'd learnt to behave himself in that most challenging of all institutions, the prison, why couldn't he control himself in the relatively benevolent real world?

Yes, the test would come soon enough, but while his mind was on the subject, yet again, why not speed things along a bit by obliging a driver to get impatient with him? There had been scarcely any cars on the lane he was on to the north-west of Stranraer, but when he finally heard a vehicle approaching he moved about four feet away from the side of the road, making it nigh on impossible for it to get by him. He also slowed down to around eight miles an hour and by pretending that he was an old chap of about eighty he remained hunched over the bars, weaving slightly from time to time, for the next ten minutes. The vehicle, which he hadn't so much as glanced at, stayed at least ten yards behind him, the driver apparently happy to bide his or her time. Carl's next problem was how to end his ridiculous performance without looking like a complete idiot, so when a farm track appeared up ahead he turned left onto it and only looked up when the car had gone past.

Resolving not to repeat that abysmal failure, he resumed his usual rhythm and soon reached the B-road that he would follow south to Portpatrick. There were a few more cars around and as the road was little wider than the lane he'd been on he was soon tempted to try his trick again, just so that he could reach the hotel having proven to himself that he could follow Christ's advice regarding those who trespass against one. For a time his chats with the C of E chaplain in his second prison had appeared to be leading him onto the path of righteousness, but when it came down to it he'd found all those miracles a bit farfetched and hadn't managed to become a believer. Even so, though most violent cons would have scorned the idea of turning the other cheek, there were certainly cases when it was expedient to do so, such as when faced with a superior opponent, when trying to secure one's release, or when attempting to carve out a new life as a roving cyclist.

With just two miles remaining and a car and caravan approaching, he couldn't resist giving it one more shot, and as the caravan was so wide he only had to ride three feet from the side to make it impossible for them to pass. This he did, and it wasn't long before the driver, who'd so far kept his distance, pipped the horn lightly. Carl grinned and put his head down, as if trying with all his might to stay ahead of them, but he kept his line and felt a thrill when the car drew gradually closer, now pipping intermittently. When the car's bumper was within just a few feet of his back wheel he was tempted to turn his head and give the impatient one a malevolent glare, but on seeing his rather scary face the driver would probably bottle it and back off, so he kept his eyes glued to the road ahead and didn't cede an inch.

Eventually it came, the great blare of the horn that made him jump despite being prepared for it, but by breathing evenly he was able to avoid losing his rag and the experiment would have proven a success had the driver reacted well to Carl's subsequent invitation to pass, once he'd steered closer to the edge of the road. He had effectively pretended to be deaf and on finally cottoning on to the presence of the vehicle, he'd pulled over, so the driver should have simply driven past and thought no more of it. What he shouldn't have done was to howl at him out of the window that he was a bloody idiot, while his wife cringed at her apoplectic husband's outburst. That was bad enough, but to then pass him by a matter of inches really was going too far. Carl kept his nerve and pressed on the pedals, but instead of roaring like a wounded lion, he took in every detail of the car and caravan before getting into its slipstream, a feat made possible by the fact that they were approaching a T-junction.

Had this scenario occurred at any time before Carl's pledge to eschew his revenge attacks, the skinny, middle-aged driver might have been dragged out of his car and subjected to a severe beating while his poor wife looked on, but the new, improved Carl Coulson simply rode right up behind the caravan and stayed there, out of sight, until the large Mercedes turned right and dragged its load briskly away, suggesting that the pilot was somewhat rattled by this strange cyclist's elusive behaviour. Had he known who he was dealing with he might have driven straight down into Portpatrick and parked near plenty of witnesses, but in his ignorance he instead turned left down a lane which signs indicated led to caravan sites. This time, however, he was in luck, because with the image of the car and caravan stored in his strangely calm mind, Carl freewheeled down the road and soon arrived at the hotel, where he put away his bike, greeted the receptionist heartily and went up to his room.

While he waited for the bath to fill, he stripped off the sweaty clothes that he'd have to rinse and dry later and thought about nothing in particular. Once submerged in the warm water he tried to think about the evening ahead, but he couldn't shut out the recent scrape for long. The caravan had been within two or three inches of him, which meant that the man was either an excellent driver hoping to shake him up or had just been lucky not to hit him. Which was it? Did it matter? As his body relaxed in the water Carl realised that he had the perfect opportunity to turn the other cheek, because if he could let that bastard off, it ought to be child's play to pardon lesser misdemeanours.

Besides, it had been his own provocation that had led to the man losing his temper, so he had to shoulder some of the blame. Hadn't that been the whole point of the exercise anyway, to incite someone to cut him up and then try to stay calm? Well, after the incident he'd acted just as he'd hoped to. He'd been observant, even memorising the number plate, and hadn't so much as stared at him. So far his behaviour had been exemplary – Mike would have been proud of him – so now all he had to do was forget about the whole thing and try to replicate that sort of self-possession the next time. He pushed himself up and out of the bath, suddenly feeling hungry. After a brief stroll around the harbour he headed for the fish and chip van and repeated his meal of the evening before, but by half past eight he was already sleepy, so he walked back to the hotel and was in bed for nine, looking forward to the next day's ride.

Carl normally slept like a log, especially after a bike ride, so it came as something of a surprise when he found himself awake at 3am. As he'd forgotten to draw the curtains he saw that the sky was already lightening and after getting up to use the bathroom he decided not to return to bed. Having already paid the bill he could skip breakfast and make a really early start for a change, he told himself, but when he sleepily pulled on his casual trousers and put on his green rain jacket over his t-shirt he saw that an early morning stroll was on the cards. After quietly slipping out of the hotel he made for the main road and headed inland for about ten minutes, before turning right down the lane to the caravan sites.

He had no specific plan of action in mind, but he wished to test his cunning by locating the caravan whose driver had endangered him and getting back to his hotel room undetected. It was nice to be out so early anyway and it had been a while since he'd seen a sunrise, so as he strolled along in his cap and sunglasses he told himself that his behaviour wasn't altogether odd. He reached the first park and was able to see two rows of caravans from the lane, so only when he reached the last one did he nip inside through a gap in the hedge to check out the rest. *His* caravan wasn't there, so he walked out of the main entrance and lengthened his stride down the lane, as the sun would soon be peeping over the hills to the east. On entering the second, larger site he slowed down and strove to look casual, though it was still so early that even the birds had yet to rise.

Towards the bottom of the site, not far from the sea, he found the blue Mercedes and large white caravan. There they were, sound asleep and at his mercy, but before walking on down to the headland he could now discern, he crept around the caravan, feeling like a kid playing at cowboys and Indians. When he found an open window into the lounge area he decided to up his game and climb inside, just for the hell of it. He got through it without making much noise and eased open the lock on the door in case he had to make a run for it. He then looked around for a pen and paper, as after all this effort it would be fun to leave them a little note. Ha, that would get their day off to a good start, when they saw that the cyclist they'd almost knocked off had been prowling around, but instead of stationery Carl was unlucky enough to find – he would later reflect – a tin of lighter fluid on a shelf.

He turned the tin around in his hand for a while and cast his mind back to the previous afternoon. Though he'd fooled around a bit on his bike, the man now asleep on the other side of the thin partition had had no right to use this damn caravan as a weapon against him. Yes, that's what he'd done, he'd put his foot to the floor and dragged the great crate past him, neither knowing nor caring if he knocked him flying! Carl unscrewed the top and squirted the fuel all over the upholstered bench nearest to the door. When the tin was empty he decided to give them one last chance. If he didn't find a lighter within a minute he would let them off and hoof it down to the sea. The smell of the fuel alone would put the fear of God into them and it was already a bit too light for bonfires, but as luck would have it he found a lighter on the table, so he felt he had no choice but to ignite the fuel and scarper.

It was fortunate that the coastal path was so close, because no sooner had he stopped running and turned to take a look than the caravan was ablaze and smoke was billowing out of the door that he'd forgotten to close. He'd assumed that caravans were more fireproof these days, but evidently not, and after rejecting the idea of waiting around to watch them jump out of the bedroom window, he walked briskly back to town, eager to get up to his room before anyone appeared. He suppressed a smile as he reached the first houses, because if anyone saw him he'd be done for, but he got back undetected, drew his curtains properly, peeled off his clothes and climbed into bed. After picturing the scene of consternation at the site, as the couple and others watched the caravan burn and melt into a toxic mess, he turned onto his side and promptly fell asleep.

9

By ten o'clock Carl was on the road to Girvan, feeling extremely ill at ease with himself. It was annoying when things didn't go as one planned and if he could have erased the events of the early morning he would have done so like a shot. On going down to breakfast at nine o'clock he'd sensed that something was amiss, as the dozen or so other guests were speaking in undertones and looking rather glum. He preferred not to ask the young waitress what was up, but by eavesdropping as he munched his cornflakes he learnt that there had been an arson attack at the caravan site and that a disabled lady had been badly burnt.

"Ach, poor woman, already suffering from MS and now this happens," one Scottish lady said to her husband, who just shook his head sadly and toyed with his bacon.

Carl was tempted to ask them what they knew, as it might not be wise to remain silent and incurious, but as he was unwilling to draw any kind of attention to himself he opted to assume the same grim expression as the others and get out of there as soon as he could. Back in his room he cursed his bad luck. That poor woman hadn't been at fault and how the hell was he to know that she was in a wheelchair? If he'd known, he wouldn't have risen at such an ungodly hour to go and carry out what was intended to be little more than a prank. It was small consolation that the husband would suffer indirectly, and when he wheeled his bike onto the street he felt like riding straight back to Castle Douglas and driving home.

This trip was supposed to open up a whole new field of activity to him, and here he was, causing havoc wherever he went. He almost wished he was back in prison, sticking to the routine and bothering no-one, but when he'd left Portpatrick behind he attempted to put the disagreeable incident behind him. Besides, the more he thought about it, the more suspicious it seemed. Surely the husband could have picked up his wife and carried her out of the door before the van caught fire. While it was true that he'd poured the fluid in the worst possible place, not having given it much thought at the time, anyone but a complete coward could have rushed through the door and onto the grass. Might the man have left her in bed on purpose? He was obviously an evil sod – he'd proved that the day before – so maybe he'd seen the chance to rid himself of a burden and start a new life. If that were the case it had certainly backfired on him, as she'd survived and lived to tell the tale, so *he* might end up in court before long, which would be ironic.

Carl had intended to bypass Stranraer and find a more rural route up to Girvan, but he was in no mood for map-reading, so he cycled through the town, oblivious to the traffic, and headed straight up the A77, riding faster than ever before. Though the coastal scenery was impressive he looked mostly at the road just ahead and the forty-odd miles passed by in a sweaty blur, landing him in Girvan much earlier than he'd intended. He liked the look of the town, especially the port area, so he checked into the first hotel he saw, stored his bike in an outhouse and undressed as soon as he reached his room. After a shower he contemplated the damp cycling gear scrunched up on the floor and considered shoving it in the bin, leaving his bike in the shed and catching a bus back to Castle Douglas. Perhaps if he put this whole cycling business behind him, bad things would stop happening, he thought as he kicked the shorts against the wall, but he couldn't do that, not after having spent the night before in Portpatrick, as the cops would already be looking for suspects.

He was almost sure that no-one had seen him in the early hours, but some insomniac might have peeped out from behind the curtains, so his best bet was to continue his tour, as it wasn't a cyclist they'd be looking for, unless that cyclist panicked and did something stupid, like leaving his expensive bike and doing a runner. No, he had no choice but to cycle on, but at least he had the whole afternoon and evening in which to be a normal tourist and try to unwind, so after rinsing his gear and hanging it up over the bath, he got dressed and headed out into the sunshine. After a bite to eat on a café terrace he considered taking a ferry trip to the nearby island of Ailsa Craig, but he didn't feel like being among so many people and instead strolled southward along the beach. It was just about warm enough to swim, as some hardy Scots were proving, but Carl settled for a paddle and it was while hitching up his shorts to wet his thighs that he saw a police car heading towards the town.

Although there was nothing odd about this and the car was just crawling along, Carl gulped and looked out to sea, though the road was a hundred yards away and there were lots of people on the beach. He reviewed the events of the previous afternoon and wondered if they might be looking for a cyclist after all. He imagined the cops asking the man if he knew who could have caused the blaze, and though a hot-headed fool like him probably had plenty of enemies, he couldn't have had time to make any in Portpatrick. He might cast his mind back and remember the foolish cyclist who he'd lost his temper with and mention him to the police on the off chance. The police might then visit the hotels in Portpatrick and ask for the names of all the cyclist guests. Carl could well be the only one, and what if they looked him up on their database?

Carl Coulson, convicted murderer.

Bingo. We've no more clues, so we'll pin it on him. He can't have got far on a bike. Where might he have headed? Somewhere with hotels. Let's get them checked out this afternoon…

Carl set off down the beach at a relaxed trot and tried to look like he was enjoying himself. On nearing the port he wiped the sand from his feet, put on his deck shoes and strolled back to the hotel.

"That's a shame," the man said when Carl told him that he'd been urgently called home.

"Yes, it looks like it's going to be a premature birth, so I'd better get back."

"We don't normally refund money if the room's already been occupied, but–"

"That's all right, I understand. Ha, maybe I'll come back when it's all over."

"In that case, the first night's already paid for."

"Thanks."

The wiry man frowned. "But how'll you get back? Where's your car?"

"It's... at home. Where can I catch a train from?"

"From here. Where to?"

"Lancashire."

"Then you'll need to go to Glasgow first. There are trains on the hour or just before."

"Great. If you could unlock the shed I'll be on my way soon."

"Right you are."

Twenty minutes later Carl was pedalling along the road heading south-east from the town. A quick look at the map had shown him that it was about sixty miles to Castle Douglas and he meant to get there by evening. That would mean doing over a hundred altogether, but he was determined to leave Scotland before nightfall. As he laboured up the sinuous road away from the coast, smiling inanely whenever a car passed, he began to think that he might be overreacting. These days the police were overstretched, what with all the cuts, so the local bobbies, if there were any, were probably still bumbling around the caravan site, ineptly questioning the other holidaymakers. In the end it all hinged on whether or not the man had remembered the incident with the cyclist, so he tried to visualise the scene from his point of view.

The cyclist up ahead, hogging the road. A couple of pips then a firm press of the horn. I yell something as we go past, but he doesn't respond at all and then seems to disappear behind us. I turn onto the lane to the site and he's no longer there.

In this light it seemed to Carl that by the time they'd got there, unhitched the van and sorted out their stuff they'd have forgotten about the incident, so why was he pedalling like mad despite already feeling fatigued after the morning's brisk ride? On cresting a rise he eased off and attempted to be honest with himself. Maybe imagining himself to be a suspect was just an excuse to cut short the trip which had gone awry since his early morning horseplay. Rather than getting so paranoid, why didn't he stay in Newton Stewart for the night and ride a different route back to Castle Douglas the following day? He then reverted to his 'worst case scenario' point of view. If the cops had already contacted the Girvan hotels and discovered that a cyclist had checked out in a hurry he really would be in the shit. A patrol car might be speeding up the road after me right now, he thought, before remembering his lucky escape from Scorton due to those fortuitous woods.

Seeing some woodland up ahead he considered hiding out again, but they turned out to be fenced off private property, so he cycled on and soon began to feel more sanguine once again. He sighed loudly and wondered if he was going out of his mind. He might be, because just a few hours after swearing to cut out the revenge attacks he'd gone and burnt down a caravan. This was hardly normal behaviour and he wondered whether he ought to see a psychiatrist or psychologist at some point. He wouldn't be able to unburden himself of his sins, of course, but by simply mentioning his irrational bouts of anger while on the bike they might come up with some suggestions, but no, doctors weren't priests and he wouldn't be able to trust them not to have a word with probation or the police. He shook his head and tried to think positively. He was well on the way to doing his first ever hundred-mile ride and that would be something to be proud of, assuming he didn't collapse from hunger or dehydration before he got back to the car.

On reaching a village called Barrhill he was about to throw caution to the wind and enter the pub, but just ahead he saw a shop, so he stocked up on pastries and soft drinks before riding on until he found a quiet lane along which he was able to gorge himself undisturbed. The sugar rush improved his frame of mind and he managed to switch off as he plodded on towards Newton Stewart, where he refuelled again before joining the dreaded A75 and embarking on the final thirty miles of his epic ride. When he finally got there, having covered an impressive 105 miles, he'd been so tired for so long that he forgot to worry about the plumber whose van he'd vandalised and before he knew it he was in the car and on the road to Gretna Green.

As he drove and sipped a can of coke he gradually began to recover and it struck him that cycling itself might hold the solution to the problem caused by that activity in the first place. When he looked back on the trip from Girvan he realised that although he'd fretted about the risk of capture for a while, he hadn't given a thought to the passing vehicles, especially on the last and worst stretch from Newton Stewart where there'd been lorries and caravans galore, all passing at fifty miles an hour or more. Generally speaking he worried about the traffic when he was fresh and forgot about it when he was knackered, so the solution might be to do really long rides in order to benumb that overactive brain of his. His grandma used to say that too much thinking was bad for you, so perhaps by doing some really exhausting rides he'd be able to go some way to straightening out those annoying kinks in his brain, caused, no doubt, by all those years of incarceration.

10

As had become his custom, Carl had a good rest after his shortened cycle tour, this time not to lay low, but to recover from the tremendous effort of that harrowing final day. For a while he was still a little worried about the caravan blaze, even keeping a small travel bag in the boot of his car which he'd filled with diesel in case he had to make a quick getaway. On the day after his return he scoured the *Galloway Gazette* and the *Daily Record* for news of the arson attack in Portpatrick and found brief articles in each that centred mainly on the woman's burns, which had been quite severe but not life threatening. The next day there was nothing new, nor the day after, so he breathed more easily again and sincerely hoped that his unintended victim would make a full recovery, although he knew from experience that burns could be nasty injuries, as his involvement in a fracas in the prison kitchen during the second year of his sentence had resulted in another con having chip pan oil poured down his chest.

Despite the unsatisfactory nature of his maiden tour, the experience had whetted his appetite and he was soon planning his next trip and ordering the gear he'd need to become a cycle camper, including a super-lightweight tent and sleeping bag, basic cooking equipment, and front panniers in which to store the extra stuff.

"Wow, you're going from strength to strength, Carl," Mike said the next time they met.

"Yes, I think cycle camping is the way forward for me. I'll normally go to campsites, so I can use the showers and wash my clothes, but it'll be nice to camp wild now and then if I get the chance."

"Scotland's your best bet then. They allow wild camping and there are plenty of places to do it."

"So do people not wild camp in England?"

"Oh, yes, though it's best to go high up on the fells, away from the farms. That's OK if you're hiking, but a bit trickier on the bike. Anyway, tell me about your last trip."

Carl told him that he'd stayed in Castle Douglas, Newton Stewart, Girvan and New Galloway, having done some research on the latter place, just in case Mike knew it.

"Sounds great."

"Yes, I liked the countryside there and most of the roads were really quiet. It was a brilliant trip but, like I say, I'm all set to go camping next time."

"Lucky you. Oh, did you not go to Portpatrick?"

Carl gulped and scratched his cheek. "Er, no. I saw it on the map, but it was a bit off my route."

"It's nice there. I used to go when I was a kid, with an uncle and aunt who had a caravan."

"Ah. How's your cycling going?"

"Fine. The good weather's meant that I haven't missed a ride since getting back from holiday."

"Oh, how was that?"

Mike shrugged and smiled. "Oh, you know, it was all right, but to go to a place like Majorca with all those mountain roads and not explore them on the bike... ha, but that's life. We can't always have things our own way. The wife didn't realise that I was pining for the roads, so we had a pretty good time."

Carl nodded and decided to get something off his chest. "Oh, when I was up near New Galloway I had a bit of a scare. A car pulled out in front of me and I had to slam on the brakes. I got really mad for a moment and felt like chasing him, but I managed to pull myself together. What would you do in a situation like that?"

"Ha, probably hurl a load of abuse at him, as long as I felt I wasn't in any danger," Mike said, before remembering where he was and who he was talking to. He cleared his throat and tried to look stern. "You, though, have to be really careful that you don't get involved in any nasty incidents. We know what you used to be like and... I don't know, a bad fright might make you... do you know what I mean?"

"Yes. Like I say, I wasn't angry for long, but, I mean, what can we *do* in situations like that? I felt really frustrated more than anything else."

"I always try to remember the reg number. Unless it's serious, like you actually get knocked off, the police can't do much, but I once used my, er... privileged position here to get the police to contact a guy who'd cut us up on the club run. They couldn't prosecute as he hadn't hit anyone, but at least he got a bollocking, which was better than nothing. They think they can get away with murder these motorists, which is why some riders have started using camera helmets."

"Yes, I've seen those. They look a bit daft, don't they?"

"Yes, and a decent one costs a bomb. One club mate's got one, which is no bad thing, but like I said once before, try not to let it worry you."

"I won't. I suppose one scare in hundreds of miles is only to be expected."

"That's right." He turned to the computer screen. "Oh, I've got some good news for you. From now on you only have to come to see me once a month."

"Great. I mean, I enjoy our chats, but I hate coming to this building."

"Yes, you tend to get a lot of unsavoury types hanging around here."

They had a good laugh about that, before Carl headed off to make the most of his thirty days of freedom.

Doing a really long trip seemed a bit daunting at first, but the more he thought about it and studied the logistics, the more sense it seemed to make. There was nothing to keep him at home and he'd be spending long enough there in the winter. Luke, his gardener, would keep an eye on the place, so there was nothing to stop him doing a four-week trip which he could always shorten if he got bored or the weather turned bad. So it was that in early July he loaded up the car and drove the three hundred miles to Oban, stopping only for a bite to eat at a service station. He parked on Longsdale carpark, which was free of charge, and spent some time arranging his stuff in his bags to achieve a balanced load. He'd put on new puncture-proof tyres for the trip and thoroughly serviced the bike, so when he wobbled off along the road he felt confident that his trusty steed wouldn't let him down on the far-flung lanes which he intended to explore.

He soon got used to the weight of the loaded bike and although the first leg of his journey towards Fort William was along a rather busy road, the scenery was so stunning that he paid little attention to the traffic. He felt great as he span the pedals and he thought that the beard he was growing made him look like a rugged pioneer and, he hoped, more worthy of respect. There were lots of caravans and motorhomes on the road, but they all took care when passing him. They too were heading up to the Highlands and islands, so he even felt a certain kinship with them and hoped they felt the same. As the tour was to be a long one he'd decided not to cover especially long distances each day and he was looking forward to spending time on campsites, where he couldn't help hoping that he might meet like-minded folk.

Yes, camping was the way to go, far better than B&Bs in towns where you then had to go and find somewhere to eat, usually paying through the nose. Carl was used to cooking for himself and he looked forward to the chores he'd have to do each day which would help to while away the time and might bring him into contact with other campers. He'd wild camp too, of course, once he got right away from it all, but in the early stages it would be good to socialise a bit and one never knew who one might meet. After stopping for a snack on the shores of Loch Linnie he pressed on to Loch Leven where he'd already chosen his destination. After a mere thirty-five miles he rolled into the Red Squirrel campsite near Glencoe where tents far outnumbered motorhomes and he was able to pitch quite near to the stream with amazing views of the mountains, including Ben Nevis.

As he expertly pitched his tiny tent, having practised in the garden at home, he greeted people as they passed and found them to be friendly and curious, as at the time he appeared to be the only cycle camper on site. Most of the other campers had a lot more home comforts than him, such as chairs, tables and awnings, but as the weather was warm and cloudy he soon made himself comfortable on the grass, leaning on his bags and waiting for the water to boil on his single gas hob. This is the life, he thought, and as there was little rain forecast during the following fortnight he intended to become at one with nature and rarely step inside a building. He'd been cooped up for too long and hoped that by getting away from the modern world he might make progress in his quest to become a more even-tempered individual.

During the afternoon he went for a short walk and after cooling his feet in the stream he settled down to read his book – about cycle touring, of course – before having a shower and setting about cooking his evening meal of pasta and a tin of chilli con carne. He intended to eat plenty of fruit every day, so he didn't worry too much about the rudimentary nature of his meals, as he'd eaten worse for many years. While he was giving the mushy mess one final blast with the gas, a woman who was walking by with a young boy stopped to say hello. She was tall, slim and looked about thirty-five. Her dark hair was tied back and though she wasn't especially pretty she had kindly brown eyes and a pleasant smile. The boy was four or five and looked sleepy.

"It must be hard work carrying all your things on the bike," she said in a southern English accent.

He smiled up at her. "Oh, it's not too bad. I take it slowly and the bike has plenty of gears."

"Where are you heading?"

"Oh, north. Once I get past Fort William I want to get off the beaten track and away from it all for a while," he said, glad that he'd grown the beard which he thought complemented his enigmatic plans.

"That sounds good."

"What about you?"

"Oh, me and Harry are on a little tour too. He's between schools at the moment, as we've just moved, so we're making the most of my holiday time," she said, crouching down and patting the grass while her son trudged off to examine the strange green coffin-like tent.

Carl thought she might have patted the grass in order to show him that she wore no wedding ring, so he stirred the food and asked her where she planned to go.

"Well, we've been here for one night already, so we might drive north tomorrow and try to find another nice site, hopefully with more kids around, as Harry gets a bit bored just with his mum, don't you, Harry?"

"No, Mum." He turned shyly to Carl. "Do you sleep in there?"

He smiled. "I'll be trying to tonight." He looked at his mother. "It's my first night, so I'll have to see how I get on in that little thing," he said, preferring not to mention that he'd already slept in it in his garden.

"We got bigger tent," said Harry, beginning to brighten up.

"I'm glad."

"We're just over there. I'm Sarah, by the way."

"I'm Carl," he said, holding out his hand, which she grasped lightly while she held his diffident gaze.

"And I'm Harry," said Harry shrilly. "My dad's got a beard too," he added, reaching out to touch Carl's.

His first instinct was to back away, as kids were something of a mystery to him and he had an inkling that they wouldn't like him, but he put on a brave face while the boy pawed his recent growth. On mentioning his dad, his mother had screwed up her nose, so Carl guessed that she was recently separated, which would explain the kid being between schools and her whisking him off to Scotland for a while. This was pure conjecture, of course, but when she invited him to pop over for a drink after dinner he had reason to believe that she felt a certain attraction towards him. It might just be that she wished to show her son that she was a free agent once more and could spend time with whoever she liked, so it wouldn't do to read too much into a simple invitation. After dinner he went off to wash the dishes and clean his teeth, before strolling over to her big blue dome tent at the appointed time.

She was seated on one of two canvas chairs with a small plastic table before her on which he saw a can of lager and an empty ashtray. Her car was an old Vauxhall Corsa, so he guessed that she wasn't well off, but that didn't matter.

"Hi," she said softly. "Harry's just got off to sleep, so we'd better keep the noise down for a while."

"OK," he murmured. "I'm not too early, am I?"

"No. Would you like a lager?"

"I… yes, please, I'll have one, though I don't drink as a rule."

"I've got a couple of cans of Fanta too."

"Oh, lager's fine. It's a nice evening, isn't it?"

"Yes, and no midges so far. I'm glad you've come over. I got a bit bored last night. To be honest I'm not really used to camping, but it seemed like the best sort of holiday for Harry, and it's cheap, of course." She opened a cool box in the outer tent, pulled out two dripping cans and handed one to Carl, who hoped she'd notice his posh watch.

"It's new to me too," he said, before giving her an abridged account of his first cycle tour.

"It sounds like you really enjoyed it, though it must be hard work. It must be good to get so much time off. I'm between jobs at the moment, until we get settled in Slough. We're going to my parents' house for a while, you see."

"Ah. I… well, I've got so much free time because I work for myself."

"Really? What do you do?"

"I'm a sort of counsellor. I work with prisoners mainly," he said. This was something he'd prepared earlier, as he suspected that the subject of work would come up and he knew plenty about counselling and prisons. "Sometimes I'm really busy, but in summer I don't tend to have much work."

"That's a shame."

"Oh, not really. To be honest, since my parents passed away and left me the house I've been all right for money." He looked at the time.

"You're not in a hurry, are you?" she said with a somewhat alluring smile.

"Not at all." He sipped the lager, which tasted incredibly strong. She'd probably had a couple already, but he would make his last, as he wanted to be on his best behaviour.

"Well, I'm afraid I've had a hard time of it recently."

Carl leant forward and nodded, encouraging her to go on, which she did, at great length, telling him all about her acrimonious marriage breakup and her hopes for a better life from now on. Being a counsellor, he only interjected the odd comment, and when she'd finally disclosed all her recent trials he managed to steer their conversation onto a more promising course. He had never married, he told her, but hoped to settle down at some point, as although he enjoyed his independence he did get lonely at times. She opened another beer and edged her chair a little closer to his. By this time, about half past ten, there were no other campers wandering around and as she became increasingly friendly, Carl tried to reciprocate in a restrained sort of way, as it had been so long since he'd been in this kind of situation with a woman that he hardly knew how to proceed. He hoped that by showing interest but keeping his distance she would make the first move, and when she eventually reached out for his hand he grasped hers tenderly and smiled, before looking shyly away.

Luckily the four or five cans of lager she'd consumed made her impatient with this coy behaviour and she was soon seated on his lap, kissing him hungrily. It felt strange at first, but he quickly got the hang of it and the canvas chair was soon in danger of collapsing due to their increasingly ardent caresses. By now there was no doubt in Carl's mind that Sarah wished to take things further, so on freeing his mouth he suggested going to his tent.

She giggled. "If we both fit in it. All right, just for a while. I'll make sure Harry's sound asleep first, then I'll come over."

Carl padded back to the tent which he now saw as a bad choice and spread his sleeping bag out on the thin mat. She soon crept in beside him and with no further preliminaries they stripped off and made love. Carl tried to last for as long as he could and when he'd finished he reckoned that he'd done reasonably well and that she'd enjoyed it almost as much as he had. After whispering sweet nothings for a while, she said she must get back to her son and began to dress.

"OK. I like it here and I don't think I'll ride anywhere tomorrow. Maybe we could spend the day together and… well, get to know each other better," he said as he stroked her hair.

"Yes, we could." She gave him a final kiss and slipped out of the tent.

Carl lay awake for some time, overjoyed that things were going his way at last. As he inhaled the unfamiliar smells he began to make plans. Being financially independent was a great boon and once he and Sarah became closer he'd think about selling the house and relocating to wherever she wished to live. He'd never tell her about his past and would have to retire from his counselling work. His money ought to last for a long time if he were careful, but he felt sure that he'd be able to think of a way to earn more once he was away from Lancashire and happy in his new life. Harry seemed like a nice kid, but he'd never try to usurp the affections of his father, who despite Sarah's bitterness sounded like a decent bloke. He opened the tent and looked at his bike in the moonlight. This holiday might not be a cycle tour, after all, he thought, before zipping up his bag and closing his eyes.

11

The sun was quite high in the sky when he awoke, feeling slightly sweaty but extremely happy. He hoped he wasn't too late for breakfast and made haste to pull on his shorts and t-shirt, before smoothing his hair and crawling out of the tent. After rinsing his face he looked over to see if Sarah and Harry were around and when he saw that the tent was no longer up he marched over, only to find that the car had gone too. His face clouded as he paced about on the flattened grass and he felt like screaming, but after stamping a ring pull into the ground he walked back to his tent and reached inside for his watch. It was only a quarter to nine, so the sneaky bitch had lost no time in clearing out. Had he been such a failure in bed last night? Had their sweet words meant nothing at all? Had she woken up and thought, 'Oh, my God, what did I do with that weird guy last night? Was I *that* pissed?' He pictured her waking up the kid and urging him to be quiet while she pulled out the pegs and threw the tent into the back of the car. The chairs and whatnot would follow and they'd be out of there within ten minutes, heading any direction but north in order to avoid that sad character who she'd taken pity on in a moment of weakness.

It might not have been like that at all, of course, but Carl was in no mood to think kindly of her just then and wished to leave the scene of his shattered dreams just as quickly as she'd done. If she'd at least left a note, explaining herself or even just thanking him for a fun evening, but there was nothing to remember her by but the lingering odour of her scent on his beard, so he stomped off to the showers to get rid of that last reminder of the bittersweet experience.

In the shower he calmed down a bit and tried to look on the bright side. He'd finally got his end away, hadn't he? And with a fairly decent woman too, though it was true that she'd seemed a bit common, drinking all that beer and going on about her ex-husband to a complete stranger, before jumping into the sack with him. No protection either, so for all he knew he might be carrying a dose of the clap. He soaped his genitals again and scrubbed them until he winced with pain. It'd serve him right if he'd caught something from the little slut and he'd be as well to steer clear of women like that from now on; all women, in fact, as they caused nothing but trouble.

Once back at the tent he decided that there was no hurry to leave after all, so he put on some water for coffee and ate a banana while he waited for it to boil. He couldn't help imagining how things might have gone with Sarah had they continued to see each other. As he sipped his coffee he remembered his absurd plans of the night before, and with a tart like that too! Had she not done a runner, it would have probably ended in disaster, especially for him, as he might have followed her down south and shacked up with her, only to realise that she was a brainless bint who would have led him a merry dance until he'd spent most of his money on her. Maybe she knew deep down that he was too good for her and that was the reason for her precipitated flight. There was the boy too. Who wants to have a kid around if he's not yours? No, she'd done him a favour by shooting off, though by doing so she'd missed out on being treated like a queen, at least until he'd realised she was no good and had extracted himself from the doomed liaison.

One good thing about the unexpected tryst, Carl mused later as he headed up the A82 towards Fort William, was that it had taken his mind off the traffic and he found that he gave all those cars and caravans scarcely a thought as he rode alongside the loch, making good time with a tailwind behind him. The further he cycled, the better he felt, and he was sure that he'd soon put his slight disappointment regarding Sarah down to experience, though a niggling feeling of anger and frustration did continue to well up inside him from time to time as he pedalled northward. His provisional plan had been to check out a campsite beyond Fort William on the shore of Loch Lochy, but he was done with campsites for the time being and ended up pressing on to the pretty village of Fort Augustus where he stopped to study his map. The deserted lanes that he craved had eluded him so far and he saw that his best bet was to tough it out on the main road almost as far as Kyle of Lochalsh, because from there a smaller road zigzagged north all the way to Ullapool.

The sinuous nature of the road and the absence of settlements of any size gave him a thrill and he resolved to get onto it that very day, even though it meant riding over eighty miles on a bike that was heavier than ever after a visit to the small supermarket. He wouldn't have minded hanging around to see if any boats came through the lock between the Caledonian Canal and Loch Ness, but the call of the wild was just too strong, so after eating a pie and a pastry he got back on the road and put his head down. He was in an exhausted state when he finally reached the longed for lane, just before the village of Auchertyre, and though it was a bit wider than he'd expected, after crawling along it for a couple of miles he had yet to see a car. It felt pretty wild up there and when he came to a large pond he left the road, wheeled his bike between some bushes and prepared to set up camp for the night, right by the water.

After pitching his tent on the flattest available spot he summoned up the energy to heat up a can of curry and butter some bread, which he wolfed down as the sun set behind him. It had been an extremely long and arduous day, but here he was, finally away from folk and enjoying his own company. You can't beat it, you really can't, he thought as he washed his face and hands in the cool water. He hoped that he wouldn't see a soul for days, and though he knew that this was unlikely, the relative isolation would do him the world of good.

'I am a rock, I am an island,' he crooned to himself as he flung his clothes to the end of the tent and finally lay down to sleep.

When he crawled out of the tent early the next morning the sight he beheld was like nothing he'd experienced before.

The pond was covered by a thin layer of mist through which the sun was slowly breaking through. As the grassy fells gradually materialised before his eyes he felt as if he were in a dream and he knew what he had to do before making breakfast. After peeling off his briefs and t-shirt he crept into the water in his walking sandals and launched himself away from the bank. Wow, it was cold! But after swimming a few rapid strokes he got used to it and was soon floating on his back about thirty yards from the shore, flicking his feet now and then to avoid going under. His ears underwater, he gazed up at the silent, evaporating mist until the blue sky appeared, upon which he paddled back to the shore and wiped himself dry. What a way to start the day, he thought as he pulled on the cycling clothes that he'd been too tired to wash. There he was, just him, his bike and enough food for several days. Who needed people when he could cycle through countryside like this and camp wherever he wished? He filled his aluminium pan from the pond and turned on his hob, before buttering some bread and hunting around for the little tubs of marmalade. His simple breakfast tasted great, as did his mug of instant coffee, and as he reclined on his bags he felt like he could stay there all morning, lazing in the sun and listening to the birds.

Just then the sound of an engine broke into his reverie and a moment later a car came along the road. He scowled and then shrugged. Oh well, there were bound to be a few pesky motorists, as the buggers got everywhere, but after consulting the map he became confident that he wouldn't see too many on his winding route through tiny villages. The odd neighbour, perhaps, but he accepted that they had the right to go and do some errands from time to time. As he was dismantling his tent another car passed and while packing his bags two more, but it was half past eight, so he guessed that some of the locals were heading off to work. He was soon on the road, riding north towards Loch Carron – more of an inlet than a loch – and during the handful of miles before he reached it four cars, a camper van and a caravan overtook him. No sooner had the stench and noise of one gone past and he was alone once more than his sensitive hearing perceived the sound of another!

Though he knew that his annoyance was irrational he just couldn't shake it off, and the eight miles alongside the loch from Stromeferry to Strathcarron turned into a series of tension-filled pauses between one vehicle and the next. He chuckled to himself – forced himself to do it – in an attempt to counter the anxiety that augmented with each pest that passed. Why wouldn't the sods leave him alone? Weren't there enough main roads in Scotland to take them to their bloody hotels and campsites? *His* road was plenty wide enough, he conceded, though there was no white line to divide the twits coming past him from the twats coming towards him, but *why* did they have to drive along it anyway? Just after Strathcarron he came to a T-junction, so he freewheeled to a halt and practically dropped the bike onto the grass verge, before pulling out his map and whipping it open. A right turn would take him towards Inverness, while a left led only to more tiny villages. Ah, maybe that was it. The dratted tourists were taking a scenic short-cut from the Kyle of Lochalsh – after polluting the Isle of Skye with their infernal vehicles – to Inverness, so if he turned left he ought to get some peace and quiet at last.

Mollified by this plausible notion, he hauled up the bike and set off towards the Applecross Peninsula, where there appeared to be only one tiny lane which meandered most of the way around it. To get to that dream road he first had to cover the nine miles to Tornapress along a similar road to the one that had annoyed him so, and though he counted a total of fourteen vehicles on that stretch, the promise of the complete solitude to come made it more bearable. Although the scenery was as marvellous as ever, Carl scarcely saw it, so determined was he to finally get off the beaten track and start looking for another wonderful camping spot near water. A stream, pond or loch would do fine, just as long as there were no damn cars around.

When he finally reached the junction he whooped with delight and practically sprinted along the lane until it became as narrow as he desired. He soon crossed a river, but no, it was far to near to the 'main' road for him to camp there, as he might hear the distant drone of vehicles and that wasn't what he'd come all this way for, so he pedalled on alongside the shallow, widening river until the road veered west and up into the green, craggy hills. The lane had passing places, he noticed, a sign that it saw little use, and during the next half hour he was alone with his thoughts; thoughts that became gradually more positive with each mile that passed.

First he reviewed his relationship with womankind and concluded once again that he was better off without them. He'd managed all right in prison, without resorting to the homosexual practices that the more weak-willed had succumbed to, so he'd shun the lot of them from now on and plough his solitary – but not lonely – furrow. He then reflected on his house and home town. Although he was attached to the old place that his parents had bought when he was about six, it was really too near to the ugly, post-industrial shithole where he'd lost his way as a youth, so the sooner he got away from there the better.

Although he hadn't passed a house for ages, he reckoned there'd be at least a hundred of them on this large and isolated peninsula, so why not buy one and settle here? They probably weren't too dear, so with the three or four hundred grand he'd get for the family home he could buy a cottage and have plenty to spare, so he definitely wouldn't have to work again. It would be sort of cool to have to drive twenty or more miles to get his shopping, but he'd cram his freezer with so much stuff that he wouldn't have to go more than once a month. He'd see no-one for days on end, but there'd be a few friendly neighbours, maybe five or six miles away, who he'd be able to visit from time to time for a good chinwag.

All this would have to wait until his period of probation finally ended, or would it? He was thinking that he'd have to ask Mike if he was allowed to move and have his appointments elsewhere – probably Inverness – when the drone of an insect proved to be no such thing. He turned his head and was astonished to see an approaching vehicle; not a car, which he could have handled, as it might be one of his future neighbours, but one of those great white motorhomes.

"Jesus Christ! Is there *nowhere* the motherfuckers don't go!" he yelled, before banging the handlebars and spitting on the road. A passing place appeared up ahead, but rather than stopping and getting shut of the interlopers, he pedalled frantically down the gentle slope in a vain attempt to leave them behind. After making it around one bend and then another by the skin of his teeth, the road tilted up and the droning motor drew ever closer. Beside himself with fury, he spotted a likely object by the roadside and stopped to pick it up, before resuming his struggle up the steepening lane. The motorhome edged nearer and the driver appeared to be waiting for the next passing place, but they were infrequent and with the sound of the diesel engine buzzing in his ears, Carl finally lost patience with his pursuers.

After rolling to a halt in the lane, he dropped the rock which he'd been balancing on his handlebars and slowly laid his bike on the asphalt. Grasping the rock, he turned to see two perplexed middle-aged faces gazing at him from the cab of their monstrous vehicle. They looked a bit foreign and he saw that the number plate was German. So much the better, he thought, before hurling the rock at the windscreen, which shattered but held fast, and with their shrieks ringing in his ears he pulled his tool from the handlebar end and scampered around the van, stabbing all the tyres. By this time they'd fallen silent, presumably petrified by this crazy cyclist's unwarranted attack, so Carl yanked open the driver's door, banged the seatbelt button and dragged the skinny, whimpering man to the ground.

A few moments earlier he could have murdered the bloke on the spot, but the hissing tyres had not exactly calmed him, but made him think a little more rationally. They'd paid for their impudence by now, so further punishment was unnecessary, but he wasn't going to make it easy for them to get back to civilisation. They'd wanted to experience the wilds of Scotland, hadn't they? Well, now they were going to stay in the middle of nowhere until some other polluting pillock came by to offer assistance. Ha, it wasn't as if they were going to die of cold or hunger in that hulking great van of theirs. They might even enjoy an evening's telly, presuming they could get a signal out there.

"Mobile phones," he hissed into the man's ear.

"What?"

"Give me your fucking mobile phones, now!"

The still supine German bleated something at his wife, who uttered a moan before producing a phone and laying it on the driver's seat.

"And the other one, you old cow!"

"There," said the man, pointing up towards the dashboard, where Carl found a smartphone tucked into a handy recess.

Not wishing to be accused of theft, he lay both phones on the road by his quivering victim and after retrieving the rock smashed them both to pieces with a ferocity that the poor couple were unlikely to forget for the remainder of their lives. After holding the rock over the man's head for a moment, he grinned and hurled it into the verge.

"Welcome to Scotland," he said, before smacking the dust from his hands and retrieving his bike.

As he powered up the slope, full of beans once more, he gave some thought to his current situation. Only a bike or motorbike could get past the stranded van, so for the time being he only had to worry about any vehicles coming towards him. Should he flag them down and tell them the road was impassable due to a broken down van? Under normal circumstances this might have done the trick, but as they'd have to drive miles and miles back to the main road were they to turn around, they may prefer to press on and wait for the van to be towed away. It might be best to get off the road and hide out for the night, but the problem with that was that come the following day the police, should they arrive, would have him pinned down in that remote spot and could even send a plane or helicopter to flush him out. This was a quandary all right, but not one that Carl found altogether disagreeable, as he'd been used to living by his wits for many years and he relished a challenge.

On reaching the top of the drag he felt one step nearer to resolving his predicament, as he saw the sea and sensed that Applecross must be just a few rapid miles away. He knew nothing about the place, except that it was small, but trusted that some kind of idea would occur to him once he arrived there. After descending at breakneck speed and enjoying every minute of it, he braked hard before a tight bend and surveyed the tiny settlement, which consisted of just a handful of properties scattered about. One, he soon saw, was an inn, but he could hardly check in for the night, so he stopped by a brown tourism sign and took out his map. To the south there lay further hamlets, but that lane appeared to end just past Toscaig, so short of escaping over the fells he'd have no way out if he took that route. Were he to press on around the peninsula he'd have to ride about forty miles before reaching the next junction, which would take him at least four hours on his loaded bike and might well lead him into a police trap.

"You're in a spot," he murmured, shaking his head and chuckling, before lamenting not having turned back where he'd brought the krauts to a precipitous halt. Had he done so, he'd have had just two possible directions in which to travel, rather like tossing a coin, but at least time would have been on his side. If he did flog himself along those forty miles to the north and east, he'd end up in the same situation, so whichever way he looked at it he was in a jam. Another option, of course, was to disappear into the hills for a few days and stay undercover until the heat was off him, but despite his recent desire to lose himself in the wilderness, when it came down to it that blasted motorhome had scuppered his quest for peace and quiet, as he'd spend the whole time fretting about being caught.

No, his only alternative was to think outside the box, as they say nowadays, and use his cunning to get far away from the scene of his latest debacle. That tourism sign indicated, among other things, that there was a campsite nearby, so he headed that way and hoped for the best. Although there were a few tents, the German couple's idea of roughing it appeared to be the most popular choice in Applecross and Carl immediately knew that one of those odious vehicles must hold the key to his escape, literally, as he suspected that the owners wouldn't be too security conscious in that remote place and surrounded by their own kind. Yes, he reckoned that at least a couple of those gas-guzzling eyesores would have the keys in or near the ignition, and he'd stolen plenty of cars in his formative years, but before he got too close an annoying impediment occurred to him, namely his bike, as how on earth was he going to get that into the back of one without being detected? He might pull it off, by frightening the alerted owners away, but as yet the Germans were the only ones who could describe him and he wished to keep it that way.

After lingering behind a bush for a while the perfect solution occurred to him, so he remounted and headed north out of the hamlet, where less than a mile away he found a wall behind which he could hide the bike and, by crouching down, himself. There he changed into his casual gear and donned his floppy hat and sunglasses, before walking back alongside the estuary to the campsite. After sauntering around for a while he was able to approach a huge Hymer whose geriatric owners were lazing about in camp chairs, but the keys were nowhere to be seen, so he moved on and perused a big grey Peugeot, with similar results. When he sidled up to a relatively scruffy VW Transporter he saw the keys near the gearstick and he'd just eased open the door when a young woman emerged from around the back of the van and accosted him.

"What the hell do you think–?" she began, but although Carl was dead against striking women he had no choice but to deliver a swift right hook to her jaw which made her slump to the ground. He didn't wait around to see if he'd KOed her, as before the count of ten he'd started the van and rolled off the pitch and onto the track, leaving the site quickly but without causing a commotion. It took him scarcely a minute to hoist the bike over the wall and shove it into the side of the van, but by the time he'd got back into the driver's seat and sped away he perceived a silver car heading towards him at great speed. He cackled, hit the gas, and was pleased to find that the van could really shift, so he was glad he hadn't borrowed one of those portacabins on wheels, as in this thing he would give them a run for their money. Although it had been many years since he'd raced around in a vehicle, usually evading the cops, he hadn't altogether lost his touch and after braking sharply to negotiate a bend before a bridge over the river he opened her up and began to distance the car, probably driven by some decrepit camper, as most of the folk he'd seen on site had been middle-aged or elderly, apart from the woman he'd slugged.

Several miles further along the coast road, however, the car kept popping in and out of view, so the driver was no slouch after all and would have to be dealt with at some point. After turning inland and driving between two small lochs, Carl reflected that he'd been lucky not to meet any oncoming cars and that now was as good a time as any to make it clear that he didn't appreciate being tailed in this way. Just before a left-hand bend he slowed to a halt in the middle of the road and waited for his pursuer to arrive, curious to see who had pitted him or herself against the most dangerous man in the Highlands since Rob Roy.

He soon saw through the mirror that the small Peugeot was piloted by a large, irate-looking man and co-piloted by a similarly enraged fellow, so rather than climbing out and pointing out the error of their ways, he waited for them to pull up some ten yards behind him, before engaging reverse gear and pressing the accelerator to the floor. They say that Volkswagens are well made, and this camper van certainly was, as in the calamitous crunch which followed, Carl sensed that the car had come off worst. Pleased with his initial effort, he sped forward twenty yards and had another bash, this time with even more deadly effect, as the car ended up sideways on and the men were both fleeing for the fields. After one more resounding wallop for good measure, he lowered his window and loudly ordered them to stop following him on pain of death, before speeding smoothly away in the structurally undamaged van, although he imagined the back end would be rather a mess by then.

"The Germans sure know how to build a van," he said, before howling with laughter. Oh, what a day it was turning out to be, and how cunningly he'd extricated himself from an extremely tight spot, he thought as he cruised along, now able to appreciate the stunning coastal scenery for the first time. Yes, he'd love to live somewhere like this, and though the Applecross Peninsula was probably out of bounds, there were plenty of other highland havens he could look into. Though tempted to wave when he did finally come face to face with a car, he instead looked down at the instant they edged past, as he felt fairly confident that there were still just three people able to identify him, unless his female victim had lost her memory on coming round from his pleasingly powerful punch. Still, it wouldn't do to be driving a stolen vehicle for longer than was necessary, so he urged her on past Shiedag and Torridon until he came to the village of Kinlochewe and a T-junction.

To the left lay Ullapool and to the right Inverness, and though he knew it was still a fifty-fifty bet and that he really ought to drive further, he manoeuvred the van behind a church and parked her facing away from a hedge so that the damage, which was considerable though mostly cosmetic, couldn't be easily seen. After pulling out his bike he popped inside to change back into his cycling gear, before slamming the side door behind him and resuming his rudely interrupted cycle tour, but not for long, as soon after leaving the village he took a right along a lane towards a nature reserve. Not far up the verdant track he climbed off the bike and pushed it through some trees until he came to a tiny clearing where he elected to bivouac for the night, the ground being too rough to pitch his tent. He'd come a long way in a day and had decided that discretion was the better part of valour and that he oughtn't to push his considerable luck by cycling onwards just yet. There was plenty of time before his next probation meeting, so spending a night or two at one with nature would do him no harm at all.

The only downside to this swift and sensible decision was that he found himself facing the evening with just three pints of water at his disposal, as once ensconced in his hideaway he didn't feel like heading off to find a stream. He drank a little and rinsed his face and hands, before pulling off his smelly cycling gear and changing back into his civvies. He reasoned that he'd need at least another pint of water to drink, so he had to choose between cooking pasta and shaving off his beard, which had become very prickly of late and was beginning to get on his nerves. He chose the latter option and as he patiently scraped away the hair with a disposable razor he admitted to himself that he'd subconsciously chosen to grow the beard because he knew that sooner or later a change of look would be advisable. Ha, it was strange how the human mind worked, his at least, and when he finally peered into his tiny plastic mirror he swore that he looked like a new man.

Was he though? Although the chase and the hammering he'd given the car had enabled him to let off a little steam, he had to confess that his behaviour that day hadn't been wholly rational. The German couple hadn't really done anything wrong, and had he allowed them to pass he could have ridden on in total tranquillity and camped at a really nice place instead of here, hemmed in by trees on bumpy ground where the dreaded midges were in evidence for the first time. He cast his mind back to the events preceding that day's strange behaviour and realised that his twenty minutes of passion with that flighty woman had warped his sensitive mind; that and the fact that she'd buggered off without saying goodbye. Yes, that was it, his first bit of nookie after so many years' abstinence had sent his neurons a bit haywire, so now he'd have to do penance by spending the night in this rotten, midge-infested hole.

So be it, he thought, and after plastering his face, neck and limbs with insect repellent he washed his hands, opened a tin of sardines, and buttered a few slices of rather limp bread. He recalled a documentary he'd once seen about ascetic monks who'd lived in the desert during the first centuries of Christianity and began to think of himself in that light. He wasn't all that spiritual, it was true, and had no plans to eat insects or flagellate himself, but a bit of hardship might do him good and help him to turn over a new leaf during the rest of his tour.

The night he spent in the dank glade proved to be just as unpleasant as he'd anticipated, as he tossed and turned on the uneven earth, waking up countless times to swat away the rapacious insects, but he must have got some sleep because come the morning he felt purged of his agitation and swore that he'd behave himself from now on. After donning his spare cycling top, a green one, and pulling on a matching helmet cover, he packed up and lugged the bike back to the track, before taking the road northwest towards Ullapool.

As his mischief of the previous day had been a bit over the top, he knew that the police in the whole of the Highlands might have been alerted, but he couldn't see there being many cops available in such a sparsely populated area, so he strove not to worry too much and just enjoy the wonderful wooded scenery as he cycled alongside Loch Maree in the cool of the morning. Each time a vehicle passed him his face assumed a serene, almost angelic expression in case that crazy bearded cyclist's antics had made the news, and on stopping at the pretty coastal village of Gairloch to rest and shop, he switched on his smartphone for the first time in a while. No, no calls or messages, so he was just as sought after as ever! He'd had a strange inkling that Mike might have called, having somehow been apprised of his favourite client's transgressions, but as he peered at the screen he chuckled on realising how improbable, not to say impossible, that was.

A quick look at *The Scotsman*, the *Inverness Courier* and the *North Star* reassured him that he hadn't made the news, so when he visited the bakery and the McColl's store he did so in a calm and cheerful frame of mind, even exchanging a bit of banter with a comely young lass in the grocer's.

On the road to Poolewe the sun came out and the stickiness he felt reminded him that he was in dire need of a soak, so on reaching Loch Tollach he found a secluded spot, stripped off, and plunged into the cool clear water, gripping a small bottle of shower gel. After performing his delightful ablutions he turned his attention to his dirty clothing and washed every single item, before laying them out on the grass to dry. After a short nap and a makeshift meal he was back on the road, resolving to cover at least seventy miles that day, which would take him within a stone's throw of Ullapool, where he intended to spend the following day and then treat himself to a proper bed for once, as he felt that he deserved a bit of comfort after... how many days on the road? On realising that it was only his fourth he marvelled at how much he'd packed into his tour so far. Not all good things, of course, but he had put all that behind him now and it was amazing to think that he still had over three weeks before he'd have to make tracks back to Lancashire. Wow, he could ride right up to the north-westernmost point of the British Isles, then head across to John O'Groats, before returning along the east coast or, if that proved monotonous, taking whichever road he pleased. Oban seemed a long way away now and his town still further, and he would have plenty to tell Mike when they next met.

As he twirled the pedals he felt he could go on forever, and though there was a big loop around to Ullapool he was sure he could reach the beginning of Loch Broom well before nightfall. All that training was finally paying off, he thought as he worked hard into a headwind, and when he reached the busier A835 the free push he received from the south-easterly breeze made the traffic seem so irrelevant that he wondered why he'd ever got so stressed about it. There was plenty of room for everybody on the Highland roads and it was fabulous to be able to stop to camp wherever one wished. For that night Carl chose a loch-side spot just short of Ardcharnich where he was able to pitch his tent and gather a few sticks and twigs to make a comforting fire beside which to eat the fried chicken and pasta salad he'd bought back in Gairloch. The few midges soon melted away into the night and he lay back to contemplate the almost full moon. Just a few months earlier he'd been lying on his prison bed, staring up at the dirty ceiling, and now here he was, under the starry sky and more content than he'd ever been. Life will be great if I make the right choices and mind my own business, he mused, and I won't let anyone, no matter how annoying they are, spoil it for me again.

12

It was misty when he awoke at half past seven the next morning, but this time rather than melt away, it thickened as he got up and prepared to leave until it had soon become an authentic fog. Prudence told him to hang around and wait for it to clear, but it was only a few miles to Ullapool where he planned to treat himself to a good breakfast with proper coffee, so he switched on his tiny LED lights and set off. Able to see about thirty yards in front of him, he pedalled slowly along, riding right on the faded white line when cars passed, but just when the fog had begun to clear he came across the first truly inconsiderate motorist of his cycling career.

A large lorry was approaching from the town when Carl heard a car coming up behind him. There was just about room for it to pass, but he assumed the driver would be polite enough to slow down until the lorry had gone by. In the event the irresponsible fool didn't decelerate enough and due to the lorry driver swerving slightly he was forced to choose between a head-on crash and passing the cyclist by inches.

Regrettably for all concerned, the driver miscalculated and clipped Carl's rear pannier, sending him tumbling onto the grass verge, where the bike flipped over and left him facing the road ahead. The driver had slowed, presumably to assess the damage he'd caused, and this enabled Carl to read the registration plate and, despite his shaken state, commit it to memory. His first impulse was to jump back on the bike and chase the car – a decrepit blue Ford Fiesta – and as he pushed himself up the driver accelerated away, no doubt relieved that he hadn't caused a serious injury, but unwilling to stick around to face the rider's evident wrath, as Carl had already shaken his fist at him and would have done much more had he caught him.

His chase was hindered, however, by an extremely sore right leg which on closer inspection he saw to be badly grazed. Whereas most cyclists would have been rightly enraged by the reckless driver, he felt remarkably calm and, rather than cycle on, he withdrew into the trees to tend to his injury and assess the situation, repeating the registration number to himself all the while. He took out his small first aid kit and while he was applying a dressing to his leg he hit upon his plan of action. As he was only about a mile from the town he decided to change his clothes and leave the bike hidden in the trees, as the business at hand would be best carried out by a non-cyclist. He checked the bike and apart from a bent mudguard which he was able to push back into place it was undamaged. After putting on his lightweight trousers, a green fleece and walking sandals, he strolled up and down among the trees until he was sure he could venture forth without limping, before donning his hat and sunglasses and setting off along the road to town.

He'd been really looking forward to reaching Ullapool and heading down to the loch shore, but in view of recent events he walked along the first street he saw and set about systematically combing the square-shaped town in search of the Ford Fiesta. Half an hour later and with only a couple of streets remaining he began to despair and thought about getting in touch with Gary, his old cellmate whose copper friends would be able to supply the driver's address, as it appeared that the man hadn't stopped in Ullapool after all and for all Carl knew might have driven off to some godforsaken hamlet in the back of beyond. On nearing the end of Seaforth Road, however, he spotted the car on the driveway of the last semi-detached house, so he walked straight past and sat down on a bench overlooking the sea loch. It was a lovely view, but Carl preferred to sit sideways on and keep an eye on the house until he'd decided how to tackle the man who had knocked him flying.

He could call the police of course, but due to the incidents of the previous day he though this unwise, as the Germans might have described his fiery blue eyes and stocky physique. In a way he was glad that he couldn't have recourse to the cops, because he preferred to do things his own way, but the question was how to determine a fitting punishment for so grave an offence against his person. The car was a rusty heap of junk, so even if he destroyed it he wouldn't hit the man's pocket very hard. Maybe he should try to catch him alone, reveal that he was the injured party and pass sentence according to how the man reacted. For a moment he began to feel quite magnanimous and thought that if the man was suitably contrite he might even let him off scot-free, which would be apt considering where he was! He had decided to turn over a new leaf, after all, so after the distress he'd inadvertently caused others, his atonement could be to pardon his assailant, if and only if he truly regretted knocking him off and driving away.

After a while he began to get a stiff neck from craning it towards the house for so long, so when a young woman emerged, got into the car and drove away, he considered knocking on the door and getting the interview out of the way, as above all he wished to put this disagreeable episode behind him and go to eat his much needed breakfast. He was adamant about getting the man alone though, and couldn't be sure there wasn't anyone else in the house, so he began to pace up and down on the grass, keeping an eye on the door almost all of the time. About an hour later his patience was finally rewarded, because a short, stout man with a balding head came out and walked towards him, so he looked away until he'd turned left and plodded off towards the harbour. Carl followed him to the ferry terminal, where he turned right and entered The Arch Inn.

Ha, he might have known that the fat clown would be a boozer, as when a man enters a pub at eleven o'clock it usually means that he's gasping for his first pint of the day. This brought the bloke down in Carl's estimation, as now that he was virtually a teetotaller he looked down on those who sought solace in the bottle. When there were so many more interesting things to do, such as cycle touring, folk who whiled away their time in pubs were beneath contempt and he doubted that someone who made a beeline for a bar on a pleasant Saturday morning, after knocking off a cyclist earlier in the day, would truly regret the sin they'd committed. As he waited on a bench some way down the street he wondered if he should risk nipping off to get something to eat, as his stomach was rumbling like mad, but just then a party of four men emerged from the pub and sat down with their pints at a picnic table outside, among them the one who Carl so wished to have a word with.

Though subdued at first, they soon became more animated and by the time the second pints had been fetched they were engaged in a lively conversation that he couldn't quite hear. From the gestures his man was making, Carl could have sworn that he was relating his amusing experience of that morning, and when he shook his fist in the air and bellowed with laughter he was sure. Feeling the rage build up inside him he began to breathe deeply, but as this had little effect he walked away along the shore, sure that the man was going nowhere fast. Words then could be dispensed with when he finally got him alone, and a good, thorough beating was what he was going to get. Carl caressed his knuckles and tried to talk himself out of it, but it was no good, this wrong had to be redressed and his escape effected before he could go on with his tour.

He thought about walking back down the main road to bring his bike closer, but just then one of the men bade the others a cheery farewell and left, so the gathering might be breaking up sooner than he'd expected. More pints appeared, however, so Carl returned to the bench and sat tight, gazing out over the loch and observing them out of the corner of his eye. Once this was over he'd be off again, north into Sutherland, where he might even find that house where he could start a new life away from people like the pissheads who were now hooting with their stupid Scottish laughter. He'd have to be careful though, so he reviewed the route back to the man's house and remembered a couple of good spots where he ought to be able to batter the bastard and make his escape, assuming there was no-one around.

Just before one the merry party finally broke up and on the corner of West Lane the other two men went straight on while Carl's quarry headed homeward, no doubt expecting to find a hearty lunch on the table. On rounding the bend onto West Terrace, however, he found himself being bundled across the street and slammed against a tree overlooking the campsite. The blinds of the house opposite were drawn, so Carl looked the man in the face, delivered four sharp blows and walked briskly away, looking back only once to see his victim slumped against the tree, clawing at the branches, looking more like a drunk than a man who'd just been attacked. Sniggering as he passed the man's house to which his wife had returned, he soon reached the main road, along which he walked purposefully, like a hiker, with a benign smile on his face.

When he finally noticed the blood on his hand he shoved it into his pocket and adopted a more casual gait. Quite when he'd decided to grasp the tool which he'd pulled from the handlebar end and pocketed, he couldn't remember, but it had made the four blows to the man's chest potentially deadly and he already regretted having thrown it away in a panic with his bloody fingerprints on it. Even the dumbest of cops would recognise where the plug had come from, so the first thing he did on returning to his bike was to pull out the other one and fling it into the undergrowth. Completely concealed from the road, he slumped down beside his bike and felt the tears well up in his eyes; not tears of contrition for what he had done, but of frustration. The equation would be dead simple this time: *fingerprints = identification = nationwide search*. He'd messed up badly and he knew it, so what the hell was he going to do now?

He was miles from Oban and his car, but even if he made it there, where would he go, now that roadside cameras could identify number plates and pass on the info at the speed of light? Going home was out of the question anyway, as unless he had an incredible stroke of luck, such as someone picking up the tool and obscuring his prints, he was done for. Back to prison he'd be going, for the rest of his life, as the justice system doesn't take kindly to repeat murderers, especially after it's spent hundreds of thousands trying to reform them. The man might not be dead, of course, but he'd felt the tool slide in right between the ribs at least twice, so he was in little doubt that he'd reached the heart, just like the last time, all those years ago, when he'd killed that evil drug dealer.

Within fifteen minutes of returning to the bike he heard the first of a series of sirens, whereupon he opened a pannier and finally had a bite to eat. After almost choking on the pastry at first, he began to eat ravenously and had soon demolished two pies and half a cake, washed down by a litre of orange juice. He felt a little better after his feast and as the sirens finally faded away he began to think more positively. They'd catch him eventually, he knew that, but it needn't be so soon if he did all that was in his power to put them off his scent. Were he to simply ride northwards as he'd planned, even if he took the remotest of roads it would be a matter of time before they nabbed him, and did he really wish to spend his last days of liberty hiding under bushes and fleeing over fells? Ha, he'd feel like Richard Hannay in *The Thirty-Nine Steps* if he did that, escaping across the Highlands after a murder he didn't commit, and though Carl wasn't quite as innocent as him, for a moment he rather fancied himself as the elusive fugitive, outwitting the filth and maybe even escaping overseas.

Not without a passport he wouldn't, so he lay down on the grass and tried a spot of lateral thinking. A stabbing in Ullapool, probably perpetrated by a cyclist, so while the police wait for a positive ID they comb the streets of the town and the roads around it. They issue warnings and as it's undoubtedly the most exciting thing that's happened around here in donkey's years everybody will have their eyes peeled. While the police search the area, possibly backed up by a helicopter from Inverness or elsewhere, all the farmers will be cleaning their shotguns and hoping to get a pot-shot at the English maniac.

What on earth was he going to do? Hmm, helicopter from Inverness... how far away is that from here? He pulled out his map and saw that about sixty miles along the main road separated him from that large town where he might be able to dump the bike and catch a train or bus somewhere. Fat chance he had of getting there. He closed his eyes and sighed. Maybe he should just give himself up and plead extreme provocation, but the knackered old car was already so battered that they wouldn't believe that his victim had ploughed into him.

For the time being it was wise to stay put, as he was so close to the scene of the crime that they might not think to examine the roadside. He crawled away and kneeled to have a pee, before lying down again. He had some food and water left, so he could make a run for it, maybe in the evening, or why not at night? He sat up and clicked his fingers. Of course, to Inverness at night! Without lights, of course, and whenever he saw a vehicle approach he'd have to get off the road. At a push he could do sixty miles in less than five hours. It was a shame that the July nights were so damn short, but if he set off at midnight he ought to have four hours of darkness, after which there'd be more roads to choose from and he could play it by ear from then on. It was worth a try, so he made himself comfortable and hoped he'd be able to doze off after his heavy meal.

Carl did sleep fitfully for a while, but it was still a long and lonely wait until nightfall. At about ten he ate again and changed into his cycling clothes, and as soon as it was completely dark he set off, as he hadn't heard a car for some time. The full moon made the road surface perfectly visible, so he soon got up to speed and had ridden a few miles when he saw lights approaching, so he skidded to halt, heaved his bike over the low barrier, dropped it and dived to the ground, hurting his injured leg in the process. As he resumed his journey he sincerely hoped there wouldn't be many more vehicles, as apart from the risk of being caught somewhere with no cover, his first evasion had been bloody painful.

"No-one said it would be easy," he murmured as he cycled along in the cool night air, and before long he was actually enjoying himself. The fact that it might be his last ever bike ride made him appreciate it all the more and he ate up the thirty miles to Garve, after which he stopped by the loch for a rest. He'd managed to evade a lorry and two more cars without much difficulty and saw that he had just twenty-five miles left to ride; less if he holed up somewhere just short of the town, as he'd decided that spending a few more hours undercover would be the wisest thing he could do. A few miles later he was able to leave the main road and approach Inverness from south of the firth, but by the time he reached Rhinduie the sun was rising and it was time to find a hiding place. Among some trees alongside the firth he lay down his bike, pulled out his sleeping bag and climbed inside. He was all in by then and if they found him snoozing away he didn't really care. At least he'd tried his best and what more could he do?

13

Half awake at about noon he lifted his hands and was relieved to find no handcuffs around his wrists. As he stretched his aching limbs he knew that he couldn't spend all day and night in that uncomfortable spot, so he might as well press on into Inverness sooner rather than later, as he'd hatched a plan which might deflect the cops and he was keen to put it into practice. A mere five miles remained for him to cycle, so he decided to do it in his normal clothes. An even shrewder move would have been to hide his bags and thus look like any old chap on a bike, but if he got out of Inverness he didn't want to come back this way, so he decided to risk it. He cycled slowly so as not to sweat too much and on nearing the town centre he coasted along, looking out for a likely pub.

It wasn't that he fancied a drink or the company of drinking men, but he knew it was in a pub where he might find the kind of person he was looking for, so on seeing a couple of unshaven louts smoking outside one housed in a fine old stone building, he locked his bike to a lamppost on the pedestrian precinct and hoped that nobody would steal his bags or spot the absence of handlebar ends, assuming his story had caused a stir this far away, which it might not have. On entering the dim interior he felt less out of place than he'd anticipated, because as well as the hardened local boozers there were also a few tourists. He ordered a pint of bitter and stayed up at the bar, on the lookout for a suitable individual, and after consuming about half of the foul brew a youngish man with tattoos came in and counted his change before ordering a pint. Being a Sunday, Carl hoped that the scruffy, tough-looking lad would have some time on his hands, so without more ado he sidled along and asked him if he could drive.

"Ye what?" he said with a scowl.

"You heard," Carl said, gazing sternly into his eyes.

"I do, yea, but what's it to you?"

"How'd you like to earn four hundred quid for a few hours' work?" Carl murmured.

The lad's eyes opened wide and narrowed again, so Carl went on. "I want you to go to Oban, pick up a car, and take it to the long stay carpark at Glasgow airport."

"Four hundred quid, ye say?"

"Yes."

"What about the tickets I'll need to get?"

"OK, I'll make it five hundred," he said, having already budgeted for the loss of over half of his remaining money, as cash machines were now out of bound to him.

"Hmm, right, and what do I do with the key?"

"You keep it. I'll be back in a couple of weeks, so I'll ask after you here."

"Fair enough, pal. Let's see the readies."

"Don't worry about that. Are you up for it?"

He looked at the clock. "Yea, I can visit my sister in Glasgow, so it's all right by me. Are you... er..."

"No questions. Come on, let's get out of here."

The lad downed his pint before following Carl outside. He explained exactly where the Volvo was parked as he slid out the wad of notes he'd folded earlier.

"Don't let me down," he said as he grasped the lad's hand and shook it firmly. "Like I say, I'll be back in about a fortnight. Who do I ask for?"

"Sam. Sam the plasterer. They've got my number in there."

"Good. Thanks and I'll see you soon," he said, almost sure that the shrewd youngster would carry out his request and might not blab too much about his strange assignment.

It was highly unlikely that he'd be returning to retrieve his key, but if or when the police found his car at the airport they'd assume he'd escaped by plane or at least headed south, as the probation services would soon confirm that he had no passport. In some ways it had been a fairly futile thing to do, but Carl knew that once they failed to find him around Ullapool they would cast their net further afield, so in the long-term, if such a thing existed for him now, it might pay off.

As it was pleasant in the town centre he decided to stay a while longer and after buying lunch in a bakery he sat down on a bench some distance from his loaded bike. It was obvious even to the dimmest mind that he ought to get rid of the bike and enjoy his last days of freedom on foot, but though he toyed with the idea of buying a large rucksack and transferring his camping gear to it, he was loath to part with the machine which had given him so much pleasure. When he was back inside at least he'd have the memories of his trips and the satisfaction of knowing that no-one who had crossed him had got away with it, least of all the Ullapool slob. Carl reluctantly switched on his phone, but before he could consult the newspapers he realised what a foolish thing he'd done and switched it off again. He hoped that those few seconds would be insufficient to trace him and thought about chucking the useless thing away, but after emitting an involuntary groan he clenched his fists and let his head fall.

After composing himself he stood up and calmly asked a lady how he could get to Oban on public transport.

"By train via Glasgow, or by bus straight there through Fort William, dear."

"Where's the bus station, please?"

"Near the train station, that way."

"Thanks," he said, before striding rapidly away.

On finding no sign of the lad at the bus station he was surprised but relieved to find him at the train station, reading a newspaper and sipping a can of coke.

"Ah, there you are."

"Aye, what's up, pal?"

"I've something else to ask of you. I want you to take this phone with you and switch it on when you leave the car at the airport. Leave it under the seat, as if I've lost it."

"The plot thickens, eh?" he said with a grin.

"If you can do that for me there'll be another five hundred quid for you when I come back. Can I rely on you?"

"Aye, I can do that."

Carl handed him the phone. "In case you're wondering, it's an... er... a matrimonial matter."

"Clearing off, eh?"

"That's right. Oh, why aren't you catching the bus?"

"Better times on the train. Don't worry, your car'll be at the airport by tonight."

"Thanks, mate."

"Aye, see you later, pal."

As Carl left the station, wiping the beads of sweat from his brow, he wondered if the stroke of luck he appeared to be having with this handy lad meant that the gods were smiling upon him at last. He was sure that when the phone was switched on the messages and missed calls would start pinging away, but he trusted that the lad would resist the temptation to look, as surely he suspected that something sinister was afoot and wouldn't wish to involve himself in it. Carl traipsed back towards the bike and called in at a newsagent's to buy a copy of the Inverness Courier. He didn't need to open it to see that a murder had been committed in Ullapool and as he strolled along he read that the police were following leads but couldn't disclose any information just yet. He pictured his bloody tool still glued into the handlebar end plug and a modern day Inspector Lestrade nimbly making the connection, before further enquiries flagged up *The Case of the Stranded Germans*. He should have worn his damn sunglasses while menacing the old kraut, but that mistake was as nothing compared to chucking away the murder weapon.

He only had himself to blame, he mused, before finally ruling out the rucksack once and for all. The road north beckoned once again and he'd cycle along it for as long as they'd let him.

14

After crossing the Cromarty Bridge some way north of Inverness he wanted to get off the busy A9 as soon as he could and the opportunity presented itself within a mile, as by way of a tiny lane he was able to join a minor road which ran almost parallel with it. Have done a £30 shop in Inverness his bike weighed a ton, but he reckoned on at least four days' autonomy before he'd have to restock his mobile larder. He had set his sights on getting past Bonar Bridge that evening, before looking for a secluded river or loch to camp beside, as he was once more badly in need of a bathe.

Although he'd be passing scarcely fifty miles from Ullapool, he was on the other side of the Highlands and so felt psychologically separated from what had happened just over a day earlier. No matter, because in a few hours his phone, whose number his friend Mike may have already given to the police, would spring into life and they'd be heading southwards as fast as their patrol cars could carry them. At least he hoped this would be the case as he cycled along under an overcast sky through rather drab moorland country. It wasn't a patch on the west coast, but it was as wild and lonely as he felt as he plodded along, the spinning pedals soothing his troubled mind. Cycling truly had proven therapeutic for him and it was a real shame that he'd inadvertently killed the Ullapool man just when he'd begun to feel calmer about the traffic.

Inadvertently? Who was he trying to kid? Although he couldn't remember having grasped his lethal tool, he certainly recalled pocketing it in the first place, and if that wasn't malice aforethought he didn't know what was. It seemed that all those years in the clink hadn't reformed him after all and that he was always destined to strike again. If he hadn't taken up cycling, would he have managed to behave himself? Probably not, as boredom would have eventually driven him back to the seamier side of life, where sooner or later another tragedy would have occurred. On reflection he realised that during his 'good' years in prison, when he'd contained his anger in an effort to prove that he was a new man, he'd merely been bottling it up for future use. When he was back inside he wouldn't do that again. No, anyone who crossed him would get it good and hard, so with any luck he'd end up segregated from the other prisoners and would get some peace and quiet at last. He might be able to continue his history studies, which he'd abandoned once he'd got out, and maybe get a proper degree, or failing that just read a lot and try to make some sense out of life.

Before he knew it he was riding alongside Dornoch Firth and on passing through Bonar Bridge he decided to cycle on to Inveran, from where a lane appeared to follow the course of a river. In the fading light he managed to find a passable spot between the trees, not a patch on the pond-side place or the lovely loch where he'd previously camped, but flat enough to pitch his tent. This was just as well, because during the night the heavens opened and Carl experienced the first sustained rain of his trip. How it hammered down on the waterproof nylon, but when he awoke it had stopped and the sun was already drying his tiny tent. While breakfasting on bread and jam he studied the map and tried to decide where exactly to head. He felt like he needed a goal to aim for, but where should that goal be? John O'Groats would be apt in some ways – the end of the country for a man at the end of his tether – but he'd heard that it was a bit of an anticlimax up there and knew that it would be full of tourists, so he decided to head north-west instead. He could go to Durness or even as far as Cape Wrath if he could get there.

It would be a fitting destination for a wrathful cyclist, but where could he go afterwards? Well, there'd be time enough to think about that once he'd covered the eighty or so miles, but he was in no hurry and opted to go north rather than north-west from Lairg, where a meandering road would take him past Loch Hope. Ha, maybe between Loch Hope and Cape Wrath he'd make up his mind what to do! Just after Lairg he found himself on the bank of Loch Shin, and as the sun was still shining he stopped to shave, bathe and do his laundry. While relaxing on the grass with a row of trees between him and the road he studied the map and decided to cycle just past a place called Altnaharra that day, from where a really tiny highroad would bring him out at Loch Hope.

When his cycling clothes were dry he set off and within two hours he was on that marvellous little road, now aiming for Loch Meadie, as it was always better to camp near water. He didn't expect to see many cars on that narrow strip of tarmac, but when he heard one approach he immediately pulled off the lane to let it pass. The lone driver nodded his thanks as he crawled by in his red Suzuki jeep and Carl smiled and nodded back, before the car accelerated away, only to roll to a halt a few hundred yards ahead of him. He cycled slowly on and saw that the weather-beaten middle-aged man – definitely a local – was speaking on the phone, so he subtly speeded up, upon which the man drove on and stopped further ahead, confirming that he'd recognised the killer cyclist – *the Psycho Cyclist*, as the papers had now christened him, but he didn't know that – and was alerting the police. Fortunately for Carl, between him and the jeep there ran a stream alongside the otherwise featureless road, so after leaning his bike on a rusty fence, still in view of the car, he ran straight into the brook and splashed along it with his head down until he could approach the car from the side.

Carl saw an excited smile on the man's ruddy face as he jabbered into the phone, glancing into the mirror from time to time, but when Carl yanked open the door his expression changed to one of terror. With his finger to his lips, Carl calmly took the phone from the man's limp hand and covered the mouthpiece.

"Tell them it's a false alarm. Tell them that and hang up."

"But…"

"And do it convincingly or I'll kill you," he said, before slowly handing him the phone.

"Er…oh, t'were a mistake o' mine. Sorry," he stuttered, before gawping at the phone.

Carl grabbed it, pressed the red button and smiled. "You didn't do that very well, did you?"

"I…"

"Get out."

No sooner had the terrified man's boots hit the ground than Carl gripped him, spun him round and wrapped his arm around his sturdy neck. During the next minute the short, rugged farmer thrashed about an awful lot, but as his lungs emptied his arms fell and his legs went limp. Carl kept pressing tenaciously until his own muscles screamed, but not until he was sure he was dead did he drop him to the road, before slumping down beside him.

"Should've minded your own business, pal," he gasped, mimicking the man's broad accent, before lying down until he'd got his breath back. He then pushed himself up and dragged the body off the road and into the stream.

Although Carl would have preferred to leave the jeep and cycle on, he knew that driving to the end of the little road made much more sense, so he opened the back door, saw there were no rear seats and shoved his bike inside, before jumping in and speeding away. The man had been speaking on the phone for quite a while before he'd reached the car, so the cops probably knew his exact position and had already alerted cars and a helicopter, so the sooner he reached the end of Loch Hope the better. There was little hope for him now though, so when he reached a T-junction half an hour later he turned left and headed around Loch Eriboll towards Durness. He expected to meet a roadblock around every bend, but the twenty miles went by without incident and he became hopeful that he might reach his destination after all, though he knew there was a tricky obstacle between the road and Cape Wrath.

He slowed to a sensible speed before entering the village of Durness, where he saw a cop standing beside his patrol car, speaking into the radio. He was looking away from the road, the fool, so Carl carried on towards the place where he hoped to find the ferry across the narrow Kyle of Durness to the cape. He had no idea what it would be like or how often it crossed, but as this was to be his final act of defiance he swore to stop and wait for the cops if he couldn't get across. There was no point heading south again, as he'd be going there soon enough, but it would be nice to reach the north-western extremity of Britain, just for the hell of it. A couple of miles beyond Durness he saw a sign to the ferry, and as he drove along the lane he spied a small boat coming across the Kyle. Surely that wasn't it, just a little motorboat? Well, even if it wasn't the ferry, they'd be taking him across if it was the last thing they did, though he hoped it wouldn't come to that.

After parking the Suzuki behind a bigger 4x4, he heaved out his bike and went to greet the chugging craft at the tiny jetty. It was piloted by a single man in a dirty yellow jacket and before he could moor up, Carl asked him if he could take him across.

"I've just taken a party across. I'll be going to collect them three hours from now."

"Er, I'm really keen to get over there," Carl said with a smile.

"But it's no good. The minibus has already gone to the cape."

"I want to cycle there."

He pulled down his hood and shook his head of greying hair. "Nay, lad, not on a bike like that you won't. It's a rough track and it's eleven miles long. I'd wait for the next minibus trip, if I were you."

"How much does the crossing cost?"

"With the bike, fifteen pounds there and back."

"I'll give you a hundred if you'll take me now."

"Eh?"

"I've got to get over soon, you see, as I'm on a tight schedule. I could come back over with the people from the minibus," he said as calmly as he could.

"Let's get the bike in then, but I'll charge you thirty, as I'm not a thief."

"Thanks, I really appreciate it. I'll be back at work in a week and I have to cram everything in."

"Aye, a lot do. Come on then."

Ten minutes later Carl was disembarking on the other side, but by the time the ferryman was half-way back across, a police car – probably the one he'd seen – came flying down the track with its siren blaring.

"Lucky for me it's just a motorboat," Carl murmured before mounting his bike and setting off along the track which wasn't as rough as he'd expected, not at first anyway, though as it gradually deteriorated he found it increasingly difficult to keep the heavy bike moving forward. After grinding to a halt on an especially stony bit, he climbed off and unhooked his panniers. He transferred a bit of food to his saddlebag and after dropping the panniers onto the grass he pressed on, soon passing another MoD sign, as it appeared that the army used the arca for training exercises. When the track turned inland it got even worse and Carl was forced to walk for a while. On spotting a police helicopter overhead he realised he probably wasn't going to make it to the cape, so when a track forked off to a beach he decided to go there instead.

The cape would be surrounded by cliffs anyway, he guessed, and he didn't really fancy that, so when he reached the small, sandy beach he was pleased by the choice he'd made. The sun was still out and the sea looked ever so blue, so he sat on the sand and began to pull off his cycling gear for the last time. It had been good while it lasted and he'd look back fondly at his numerous trips when he was back behind bars. The helicopter was circling by now and he hoped it wouldn't land just yet, as he wished to enjoy his last bit of freedom for a while longer, so when it flew off to the south he exhaled contentedly and decided to go for a swim. The water was cold but the waves not too high, so he swam out until he could still stand on tiptoes. He looked out at the ocean that stretched away to the arctic and back at the golden beach. This is a nice way to end my trip, he was thinking when he saw dust rising from the track. He first heard then saw two army jeeps coming towards him at speed, so he sighed, turned, and began to swim strongly out to sea.

THE END

Printed in Poland
by Amazon Fulfillment
Poland Sp. z o.o., Wrocław